THREE-STAR CUISINE

THREE-STAR CUISINE

a nobleman in the kitchen

BOMER VON MARX

with an introduction and wine suggestions
by Bruno Caravaggi and Gino Robusti

H JAMES H. HEINEMAN, INC., PUBLISHERS

First Printing 1965

Library of Congress Catalogue Card Number: 65-24534

For information address: James H. Heineman, 60 East 42nd Street,
New York, New York 10017.
Printed and bound in the United States of America

TO FRANCES ANNE

contents

why the book?

The real joy of this book, not only to the publisher but to all who relish fine food, is that each person who has had a hand in it is a professional of long standing, accepted as a top-ranking artist in his or her particular field. There is, of course, first the author, Bomer von Marx, a man who has lived on both sides of the kitchen door. He has lived in the kitchen as a chef, and he has lived in the drawing rooms and dining rooms as a squire. Born to the manor, his homes on both sides of the Atlantic have been redolent with the cheer that good food, wine and company can bring. Since his earliest youth he has enjoyed the best in quiet luxury while dining in the mansions of friends and in three-star restaurants and hotels throughout much of the civilized world. In a profession that is subjected to continuous critique, he has reached and maintained a position of the highest rank as chef, restaurateur, cooking school director and epicurean scholar. As a man who knows the food business from top to bottom, who is long experienced at producing and purveying the best of *haute cuisine,* and who is gifted with one of the most refined tastes in his profession, von Marx brings to the book a wealth of practical cooking knowledge never before presented in a single volume.

His practical professionalism is exceeded only by his ebullient artistry and imagination in the preparation of food and by the enthusiasm he has brought to each of the recipes, tenderly chosen, lovingly perfected and carefully worded.

The selection of wines, ever a challenge, has been assigned to two other gifted professionals. Gino Robusti and Bruno Caravaggi have been restaurateurs for most of their lives. They earned their reputations at Western Europe's finest tables, climaxing their careers by opening one of New York City's most celebrated restaurants, Quo Vadis, which they have been operating to the delight of gourmets for some twenty years. Every day of their long and accomplished career has been spent in the happy process of blending food, wine and people to the maximum advantage of all three.

As for the editing of this stimulating volume, Miss Helen McCulley, food editor of *McCall's* for some thirteen years and presently one of the country's most sought-after food consultants, has left nothing to chance in combing through the text with an eye sharpened by the critical evaluation of hundreds of articles, columns and books. It must be agreed, however, that her task has been made easier by one important fact: Every recipe in this book has been tested and proven literally thousands of times—both in restaurants and in homes—on diners, around the globe, many of whom are possessors of the most exacting palates in existence. The wine suggestions, too, have been proposed hundreds of times, usually with the most gratifying results.

Carrying the entire book assignment to professional conclusion, the publisher contracted for the services of Leo Glueckselig for the art-work and Norma Levarie for the volume's overall design. Schooled as an architect in Vienna, Mr. Glueckselig perfected his art as an illustrator and has been a contributor to leading magazines and books in the United States. Miss Levarie, whose book designs and jackets grace thousands of home and library shelves, is also noted as a creator of fine designs for Corning Glass.

Why all this emphasis on professional perfection, to the point where some may feel that the publisher has lost his truffles?

The objective is quite simple: An avid yearning to produce a book that cannot help but make an ordinary cook into a good one and a good cook into a superb one. The formula, too, is quite basic: The idea that it takes a blending of professional practicality, imaginative enthusiasm and loving devotion to prepare inspired meals. Cooking is really the only art that is rendered with the idea of pleasing everyone, whether it be two people in intimate reverie or two hundred at an elegant banquet of state. Though other arts must seek the lowest common denominator to please the masses, cooking stands alone in reaching them through the highest common denominator, perfection.

The Tender Loving Care that has gone into each element of THREE-STAR CUISINE is part of that highest common denominator, an essence that can lead more and more people to a better and better enjoyment of fine food and drink.

Yet do not be alarmed into misconceiving this book to be aimed at the dedicated gourmet alone. On the contrary, the very professionalism that has gone into every step of its preparation has tailored the recipes for the homes of cooks of all kinds who live in today's fashion—servant-less, pressed for time, limited by household budgets and relentlessly devoted to the rigors of waistline-watching.

This book is for all those who enjoy cooking, who smile warmly at the very thought of good food, and who realize full well that you never get old around the table.

JAMES H. HEINEMAN, *Publisher*

NEW YORK CITY
NOVEMBER, 1965

preface

It has been said that a good cook can make much out of nothing, while a bad cook can make nothing out of much. It is indeed a sad thing to hear about meals that have been ill prepared, for there is really no reason at all why almost any one on earth who so desires cannot be a good cook. The preparation of food is an art that derives from a blending of such intangible qualities as taste and temperament. Yet it is also, happily, a realistic art, since any cook can come up with an excellent meal if he or she will pay full attention to the recipes and follow them conscientiously.

Good cooking also requires a quality which is helpful to almost any area of human endeavor: *enthusiasm*. Fortunately it is easy to maintain enthusiasm when preparing a meal because the preparation time from start to finish is short—or relatively so in comparison with other fields of creativity. In how many of the arts can a person behold the outcome and experience, the thrill of accomplishment in a matter of only an hour or two? In painting, you can hardly set up your easel and mix colors in that amount of time. In writing, you may barely have produced two or three pages of rough text. In music, you would be lucky to have established the beginning of a theme.

No, only in the art of cooking can achievement take place so quickly, so spontaneously, so satisfactorily.

There is a certain formula, it is true, in the successful preparation of a recipe or an entire meal. You might say that good cooking depends in its physical aspects upon three things: sight, succulence and service. The dish itself must have an appetizing appearance; the food must have the proper preparation to give it the right degree of body, texture and fragrance; and the whole must be presented to the diner in a pleasing, relaxed manner and in a congenial setting. All my life, though, I have been practicing a more simple and direct formula in my association with food: *love.* Love will see to it that the ingredients are selected and measured with care; that they are tenderly subjected to the manifold processes of preparation and cooking; and that they are served at exactly the right moment, in the right manner, to the right people. If you are wondering about your abilities as a cook, you will find that love—or just plain affection—will generate quite naturally those other qualities: enthusiasm, attention and a desire for perfection.

I have never known persons who liked to cook who were poor cooks. On the contrary, most of them were excellent ones. We all understand that good recipes help to make good meals. But cooking is such a personal and subjective activity that real achievement can be attained only when the use of a good recipe is accompanied by an honest enjoyment in working with it.

One condition that all beings regularly share—man and animal alike—is hunger. What separates common man from the beast and superior man from common man is the manner in which he satisfies that craving: Either with a rush to ease the physical pangs within the stomach, or artistically, imaginatively, creatively in a way that brings intellectual and emotional, as well as bodily, enjoyment. We eat basically because we must, and unfortunately many people cook for the same reason, with a feeling that the whole process is a chore to be discharged as rapidly and as painlessly as possible. Yet there is no limitation to what *any* cook can accomplish if he will, nor to the satisfaction and rewards he can enjoy through his endeavors.

location and altitude. So the loving cook simply observes, keeps his patience and learns through experience just when the food under preparation has reached its savory zenith.

Besides possessing the most important ingredient of all, the honest desire to get the most out of a recipe, the successful cook devotes undivided attention to the step-by-step progress of the meal. He tries to arrange his schedule so that there will be a minimum of interruption. It is almost unnecessary to mention that he has already selected the best quality ingredients that he can afford, and that he will take great pains to avoid the error that has inadvertently sabotaged many a cook: *overseasoning*. He knows that the addition of extra wine or more butter than called for does not necessarily achieve the richness desired, and that in fact such misguided generosity may prove cloying to the taste.

I have prepared each chapter with the inclusion of a brief introduction that contains general guidelines. This passage will assist you in giving thought to a better planning of your menu before you begin, taking into account the nature of the recipes you may consider, the kind and number of guests, the climate and season, the occasion and other pertinent factors. The most important section to consider —it need hardly be said—is the individual recipe.

My hope is that you will experience even a small fraction of the pleasure in the cooking that I have enjoyed in the writing. Good eating is essential to good living. And both are available to anyone who values fine food enough to cook carefully, intelligently, enthusiastically—and with loving care.

BOMER VON MARX

PARIS
OCTOBER, 1965

THREE-STAR CUISINE

Drink
thy Wine
with a
Merry Heart

a word about wines

"Les goûts et les couleurs ne se discutent pas."
To say that "tastes and colors cannot be discussed" does not quite interpret the full meaning of the Gallic original. But perhaps it does get across the idea, which our experience appreciates, that some things cannot be dictated. Nevertheless, we are sticking out our necks. One cannot be dictatorial with wines. Yet we shall tell you in this book what wines we would select for the fuller gratification of each course. We qualify this. We are not intractable. We have only selected wines in respect to what we ourselves have known and enjoyed for years—how many years we do not wish to admit. Well, we will admit that for more than three decades it has been our professional art to recommend these wines with the dishes in this convivial book. Our duty and our pleasure has been to know wines. And to know more: the guests, the occasion, the emotional setting. One might say that we are conductors. We have been orchestrating food, wine and people all this time, bringing the three together into what has most often been a gratifying harmony.
We know the mood of the dishes because we know the ingredients and the recipes and what the chef is doing in the kitchen. We know

the wine because we know the grape and where and how each bottle has come into being.

What we cannot know in this too-impersonal world of print is *you.* We are therefore presumptuous in assuming that since you are reading this book, you relish fine eating—that you find an exuberance in the offerings of a good table. As the French quotation above suggests, we cannot argue taste any more than we can tell you to prefer a red candle to a green one, a blue flower to a yellow one, Colombian coffee to oolong tea.

Yet we will be positive about this subject that is dear to us. To him who will question any of our selections we shall say, "We have come to our opinions through many years of experience. Who is to say we are right? Well, who is to say someone else would be more right?"

The table should be a place of accord. Diplomats from many nations may argue hotly over many issues without reaching agreement on any one. They may not even see eye to eye on the meaning of peace. But these people can ultimately sit down together at the dinner table and agree on one thing: that fine food, good drink and an able cook are highly desirable elements in this world. This is not to say that the man who prefers Dover sole will concur readily in detail with the man who prefers Wiener schnitzel. But both will agree that perfection in preparation is a highly desirable quality to have.

Sometimes, though, the table is a powerful instrument of accord. The French have another expression. They say that all big decisions are made between the cheese course and the fruit course. Or, as they say it, *entre le fromage et la poire.*

But, to get back to the wine . . .

There is a bottle just for you, for the menu, the occasion, the mood. We are trying to help you seek it out. How did we go about choosing our wines? Our first purpose was to provide an agreeable variety, to give numerous wine-producing countries a chance to show that quality is an international essence.

Courage has led us to name selections. Experience has advised us to name alternates.

You will notice that we have selected the type of wine, such as Bordeaux or Burgundy, but without specifying the year, the growth or the vineyard. Why? Because you can best seek that special information when you visit your wine merchant or make a selection from the sommelier. Just as you will determine what butter you are going to buy, or what brand of spice. We have chosen those wines that we feel are generally available, that are not too rare, and that are in most cases reasonably priced. What a disaster it would be were you to select your menu with devotion and enthusiasm—only to find that you could not locate a compatible wine! Or that its high price would necessitate skimping on other parts of the meal!

This book might have been entitled *The Making of a Gourmet* because of the care and knowledge that have gone into the selection and composition of the many superb recipes. We hope that our own devotion in recommending the wines as accompaniments to recipes which, we well know, will add immeasurably to the enjoyment of fine cooking that lies within your everyday reach.

Les goûts et les couleurs . . .

Who is to say?

BRUNO CARAVAGGI
GINO ROBUSTI

QUO VADIS RESTAURANT
NEW YORK CITY
OCTOBER, 1965

sauces and basic preparations

Sauces are the
most significant test
of the skill of any cook.
They represent the top art in
culinary achievement
and require great exactness
and consummate finesse. Foods
served without any kind of sauce
are completely appropriate only for
those on very strict diets; for sauces

make any meal more complete and delicious. Fine foods deserve and require fine sauces to complement and heighten the desired effects. Sauces may be classified in four categories:

1) JUICES. These include meat stock, vegetable stock, fish stock, chicken stock, and basic brown sauce. These juices should be completely fatless. Gravy with fat is bad cooking. The fat spoils the taste because hot fat closes the pores of the tongue and leaves a bad aftertaste.

2) THICKENED SAUCES. Such sauces are made with egg, cream, or butter as a thickening agent.

3) VELOUTÉS AND BÉCHAMEL. These sauces are made with meat, vegetable, fish or chicken stock and milk, and are thickened with flour.

4) PURÉES. These are prepared from vegetables, fruits, meat or fowl.

Study the recipes in this chapter carefully. Some of the sauces may be made in large quantities and stored for a very long period of time (basic brown sauce, for example) others will keep for a few days only; still others must be made-up fresh each time they are served, but these are usually sauces which require a minimum of cooking time.

The recipes in this chapter deserve your closest attention. Properly prepared, they provide the best possible showcase of your cooking prowess.

ASPIC

Into a large kettle put 4 quarts of water. Add 2 pounds lean beef (least expensive cut, cut in cubes); 2 pigs' feet, chopped; 3 calves'

feet, chopped. Cook 4 hours. Then add salt, pepper, ¼ cup vinegar, ½ cup dry white or red wine, 2 bay leaves, ¼ teaspoon thyme, parsley sprigs, celery, tomatoes, carrots, leeks, and simmer another 3 to 4 hours. Strain and allow liquid to cool.
Return to heat and when liquid is almost to the boiling point, beat in 4 stiffly-beaten egg whites, the crushed shells of the eggs and a little lemon juice. Beat constantly with a wire whisk until boiling point is reached. Boil 5 to 10 minutes, then remove from heat and cool completely. Strain through a cheesecloth without pressing. At this point you have a crystal-clear, concentrated, liquid aspic which will solidify when refrigerated. Its refrigerator life is about 3 weeks. Before using, reheat and add a little sherry, port, or red wine.

NOTE: For small quantities, canned aspic (meat jelly) flavored, if necessary, with a little port, sherry, or red wine can be used.

BARQUETTES

Sift 2½ cups flour together with a pinch of salt. Cut in a generous ½ cup (1 stick) butter and stir until mixture looks mealy. With a fork stir in a mixture of 1 egg, 1 additional egg yolk, and 2 tablespoons cold water. Work pastry lightly and gather together in a ball. Press a thin layer on the bottom and around the sides of well-greased, small, oval tart pans (these are called barquettes). Prick pastry on bottom with a fork and fill each barquette with a small handful of dried beans or peas. This prevents the bottom from puffing up and the sides from collapsing. When mixture is well-browned, remove beans and peas.

BÉCHAMEL

This is made exactly like Velouté (page 28), but with one difference: Hot milk is used in place of hot stock.

BEURRE MANIÉ

This is a good way to thicken a sauce, gravy, or stew. Take 1 tablespoon soft butter and work into it as much flour as the butter can hold. Drop small pieces of it, bit by bit, into the boiling liquid which you wish to thicken. Stir constantly with a wire whisk until right consistency is reached.

BASIC BROWN SAUCE

This recipe makes a strong, dark, tasty, and completely fatless gravy. Used as a base, it can be made into different sauces by adding other ingredients and flavorings: Sherry, port wine, brandy, tomato purée, cream, herbs . . . to name only a few.
Start off with a medium-sized roast of veal or beef (about 3 to 4 pounds). Heat 4 tablespoons of butter in a casserole until brown, then add plenty of sliced carrots, 2 to 3 large sliced onions, 2 pounds of chopped bones (veal or lean veal knucklebones are best), add 2 to 3 tablespoons of oil. Cook until vegetables and bones are a rich brown in color. Add the roast and brown on all sides. Add consommé to about one-third the height of the roast. Cover pot, bring to boil, and cook in oven at about 325° F until roast is tender. The liquid should just simmer during this time. Remove roast from pot

and serve hot or cold, but without gravy when you apply this method of cooking.
To the vegetables and bones in the pot, add a few more cups of consommé, scrape down all brown residue from the sides and bottom, and let simmer for another 30 minutes with the lid on. Work through a strainer into a bowl, pressing out all the liquid. Refrigerate. The next day the fat will form a solid layer over a rich brown liquid, and this can be refrigerated for as long as several months.

CRÊPES

Heat 2 cups milk until a film shines on top. Set aside to cool.
Mix together 3 to 4 tablespoons flour, a pinch of salt, 3 eggs plus 1 additional egg yolk and the hot milk. Beat together thoroughly, and set aside for about 1 hour, then work the batter through a strainer and stir in 2 tablespoons whipped cream. The consistency of the crêpe batter is very important. A good test is when butter runs off wooden spoon like a string.
Take a shallow iron frying pan, one about 6 inches in diameter, add a little butter and heat through. *Remove from fire,* pour in just enough batter to cover the bottom and swivel the pan to distribute it evenly. Cook over a medium heat, loosening the edges with a spatula. When nicely browned, turn crêpe over and brown second side (for the record, your first crêpe never turns out perfectly—the pan must have reached its right degree of heat). Make up all remaining batter. You will notice that, except for the first crêpe you made, practically no additional butter is needed in the pan. If crêpes are not to be used immediately, stack them on top of each other with a sprinkling of confectioners' sugar between. Wrap the stack in a dry cloth and refrigerate. They can be made 1 or 2 days in advance.

DRESSING FOR GREEN SALAD

Most people have their own ways for preparing salad dressing, therefore this is only a suggestion. Combine 1 tablespoon tarragon vinegar, 3 tablespoons salad oil, 1 tablespoon French mustard (preferably French herb mustard) or somewhat less, ½ teaspoon sugar, salt to taste. Rub the bowl slightly with garlic before adding any of the salad dressing ingredients. Toss the salad well and sprinkle with chopped tarragon and chives.

FONDANT

Moisten 1 cup sugar with a little water. Add a few drops of vinegar and cook over a low heat, stirring constantly; until syrup drops as a thread from your spoon. Pour the hot syrup onto a marble or metal-topped table and let it get cold. With a spatula work the mixture until it takes on a white color and becomes very thick. Scrape fondant off the work surface with spatula and knead it with your hand until soft and creamy. Shape into a ball, place in an airtight container and refrigerate.
This ball of fondant will keep for a month or 2 in your refrigerator. Portions can be used when needed.

TO USE FONDANT: Over a low flame heat some of the fondant with melted chocolate, a few drops of water and a little oil or melted butter. Stir constantly. When fondant is of pouring consistency, spread over cake. Other flavors such as liqueurs, cognac, rum, and coffee can be used. If chocolate is not used, the fondant can be colored by adding a few drops of food coloring.

sauces and basic preparations

FORCEMEAT OF CHICKEN [QUENELLES]

Remove crusts from 6 slices white bread, soak bread in milk, then squeeze dry. Combine with 2 large, raw chicken breasts (skin, bones, and sinews removed), 2 to 3 tablespoons butter, 2 egg yolks, 1 whole egg, pinch of nutmeg, salt, and pepper. Work mixture through a food grinder, using the finest blade, several times. Shape into little mounds with a spoon or push the mixture through a pastry bag with a large tube and slice according to size you wish. Drop into simmering consommé. When quenelles float on top, they are ready to use; lift out with a slotted spoon.

FORCEMEAT OF VEAL [QUENELLES]

Heat butter and water together to the boiling point. Stir in flour, all at one time. Cook until paste is smooth and thick. Remove from heat, cool, and add very finely-minced veal. Work mixture thoroughly with your hand. Add eggs, 1 at a time, and work again. Press mixture through a sieve. Shape into mounds, with a spoon, the size called for in given recipes, and drop into simmering consommé. When quenelles float on top, they are ready to use; lift out with a slotted spoon.

½ cup [1 stick] butter
1¾ cups water
1 cup flour
1¼ pounds lean veal
3 eggs
Consommé

CHOCOLATE ICING

Melt 5 squares (5 ounces) unsweetened chocolate over hot water. As it melts, add ½ tablespoon butter.
Moisten 1 cup sugar with a little water. Cook over low heat, stirring constantly, until syrup drops as a thread from your spoon. Stir syrup into chocolate quickly, adding a little more butter. If icing gets too thick, add a few drops of hot water. Spread over cake with a spatula.

LOBSTER BUTTER

Mash or chop the shells as fine as possible, then put them through the food grinder once. Melt butter in a large frying pan (do not brown). Add shells and paprika. Fry about 5 to 10 minutes, then stir in cognac and ignite. When flame dies away, add a few drops of red food coloring and simmer for another 20 minutes. Press mixture through a fine sieve or strainer thoroughly. Discard shells, refrigerate the liquid. Next day spoon off the top layer of the solid red lobster butter and discard the liquid beneath. Lobster butter will keep indefinitely in the freezing compartment of the refrigerator. Needless to say you can double or triple the quantity.

4 cups cooked shells, especially heads and claws of lobster, langoustine, or crayfish
1½ pounds butter
2 to 3 tablespoons paprika
½ cup cognac
Red food coloring

sauces and basic preparations

MAYONNAISE

Put 2 or 3 very fresh egg yolks in a bowl. Stir in ½ tablespoon French mustard thoroughly. Start adding oil, a few drops at a time, beating continuously with a wire whisk. Beat in enough lemon juice or vinegar, salt and pepper to please your taste. If a very light mayonnaise is desired, mix in some whipped cream.

CURRY MAYONNAISE

Dissolve some curry powder in a little cold consommé and stir into mayonnaise (see above).

PASTE FOR CREAM PUFFS AND ÉCLAIRS

Put ¾ cup of water, a pinch salt and 3 tablespoons butter in a saucepan. Cook until water boils and butter has melted. Remove from heat, stir in ½ cup flour all at one time and mix. Return to heat and stir with a wooden spoon until mixture thickens, pulls away from the side of the pan, and forms a ball. Remove from heat and beat in 2 eggs, 1 at a time. Hard, constant beating is essential. Dough should be thick, smooth and shiny.
Place dough in a pastry bag and pipe little mounds, allowing space for expansion, onto a greased baking sheet. These make the characteristic cream puff shape.
Bake in a preheated 425°F oven. Leave oven door slightly open to

allow steam to escape. The puffs are done when they have doubled in size and have a firm, golden-brown crust.
To pipe éclairs, draw the paste along for about 3 to 4 inches. Brush tops with well-beaten egg. Then pull the tines of a fork lightly down the length of each éclair.

PASTE GÉNOISE

Mix sugar and eggs and beat over a small flame with wire whisk until mixture becomes twice as thick. Then remove from stove. Add the flour, little by little, and mix well. Then add, also little by little, the melted butter, cooled. Spread about ¼ of an inch thick on a buttered and lightly floured baking tin. Bake in a preheated 350°F oven for about 25 minutes or until cake pulls away from the sides of the pan.

½ cup plus 2 tablespoons sugar
4 eggs
⅔ cup flour
7 tablespoons butter, melted

PASTRY BRISÉE

Sift 2 cups flour, 1 tablespoon sugar, and a pinch of salt into a bowl. Cut into ½ cup butter [1 stick] until mealy. With a fork work in a little cold water (about 2 to 3 tablespoons). Gather pastry together in a ball, wrap in wax paper or a cloth and refrigerate about 2 hours. Knead lightly before rolling it out.

PASTRY FOR FRUIT TARTS

Mix ¼ cup flour with ¼ cup sugar, then work into it ½ cup [1 stick] butter and 1 egg yolk. Work well with the heel of your hand, then gather dough together into a ball and refrigerate for about 1 hour. Roll on a lightly floured board and line a greased tart or pie pan. Bake in a preheated 350°F oven until set (in other words, half-baked). Remove from oven and arrange fruit on top. Return to oven and continue baking until pastry is nicely browned.

PASTRY SUCRÉE

Mix ¼ cup sugar, a pinch salt, 1 whole egg, and 2 egg yolks together thoroughly. Then work in ¼ cup [½ stick] butter and 1 cup flour. Let the pastry rest for 1 hour before using. This dough is especially recommended for fruit tarts.

CRÈME PÂTISSIÈRE

Heat 2 cups milk with a vanilla bean until a film shows on the surface. Beat 4 egg yolks with ½ cup sugar in an electric beater until mixture drops like a string from a spoon. Add 1 cup flour and beat until smooth. Stir in the hot milk thoroughly. Return to stove and beat constantly with a wire whisk until mixture thickens and boils for about 5 minutes. Remove from heat and cool.
Crème pâtissière can be used immediately as a filling for cream puffs (page 15) or éclairs (page 15), or as a base for soufflés (page 220), or it can be refrigerated and used when needed. It will keep satisfactorily for 4 to 5 days.

SABAYON

Sabayon is used mostly in combination with any Velouté (page 28). Mix together 2 cups consommé, 1 cup dry white wine, chopped onion. Cook over a moderate heat until liquid is reduced to half. Strain and beat in 3 to 4 egg yolks. Yolks should be added while liquid is off the stove.

SAUCE AMÉRICAINE

Take 2 tablespoons Lobster Butter (page 14) in place of fresh butter and make a Velouté (page 28) with fish stock. Add grated onion, ½ tablespoon cognac, salt, pepper, paprika, 2 tablespoons Basic Brown Sauce (page 10). Let simmer for about 10 minutes and strain. Put back on the fire, add ½ tablespoon lobster butter and ½ cup cream mixed with 1 egg yolk. Taste for seasoning.

sauces and basic preparations

BÉARNAISE SAUCE

This sauce, belonging to the Hollandaise group, must be carefully made over a very low heat, otherwise it will curdle.
Combine 2 cups consommé, 1½ tablespoons vinegar, ½ cup dry white wine, 2 tablespoons chopped onion, salt, and pepper. Place this mixture over fire, bring to boil and reduce it to half. Strain. Remove from fire and cool. Add 3 to 4 egg yolks, 1 at a time, beating them into the cooled liquid. Then replace over a very small flame, beating constantly with a wire whisk until the sauce thickens considerably. Again remove from flame and, while still warm, add about 4 to 5 tablespoons melted butter, cooled, little by little, beating constantly. Also a few drops of Worcestershire sauce, plenty of chopped tarragon and parsley, salt, and pepper.
If the sauce is to be served with vegetables or fish, add lemon juice; if used with red meat, add tarragon vinegar and 1 or 2 teaspoons Basic Brown Sauce (page 10).
This sauce, which can be kept until needed in a double boiler over hot water, is served tepid.

SAUCE BORDELAISE

Combine ½ bottle dry red wine, 1 finely chopped onion, 2 cups of Basic Brown Sauce (page 10), 1 crushed bay leaf, sprig of thyme, 3 ripe tomatoes, sliced. Cook to a boil, then simmer for about 30 minutes or until liquid has reduced. Taste for seasoning and, if necessary, thicken with a little Beurre Manié (page 10).

HOT CAPER SAUCE

Make a Velouté (page 28) with mushroom or fish stock or consommé [the purpose of the sauce will determine the stock]. Add a little vinegar, salt and pepper, an ample amount of drained capers and a little cream. French mustard is optional.

BROWN CHAUD-FROID SAUCE

Follow the recipe for White Chaud-froid Sauce (page 20), but make the Velouté (page 28) with Basic Brown Sauce (page 10) instead of consommé, and use port wine instead of white.

WHITE CHAUD-FROID SAUCE

Make a Velouté (page 28) with chicken or mushroom stock. Soften a little unflavored gelatin in a little cold water, then stir into the hot Velouté along with a little dry white wine, cream mixed with 1 egg yolk, salt, and white pepper, if needed. Work through a sieve and, while still hot, stir in a little Aspic (page 8).
Use as coating for cold whole chickens or chicken breasts or mousses.

CHOCOLATE SAUCE

Melt 8 squares (8 ounces) unsweetened chocolate over hot, not boiling, water. Combine with light cream and sugar to taste. If too thick, stir in a little more cream while sauce is still hot.

sauces and basic preparations

CHORIZO SAUCE

Chop Chorizo (a very spicy, dried Spanish sausage) very fine and combine with chopped cheese and a little cream. Heat until cheese melts and sauce blends together. Use as a sauce with meat or over foods you wish to serve *au gratin*.

SPECIAL SAUCE FOR COCKTAILS

In a bowl combine Mayonnaise (page 15) with ketchup, some Worcestershire sauce, a bit of onion juice, several drops of Tabasco, a little lemon juice and grapefruit juice, some finely chopped parsley and tarragon, a touch of horseradish or dill, dash of port wine and Grand Marnier. Place in a bowl of crushed ice and serve with cold shrimp, lobster, crayfish, and the like.

CREAM SAUCE FOR ROASTS

Take Basic Brown Sauce (page 10) and bring to boil. Add salt and pepper, a few drops lemon juice, purée of tomato, tarragon leaves (optional), then reduce and strain. Reheat, adding heavy cream and raw yolk of eggs, but do not boil.

CUMBERLAND SAUCE

Empty 1 jar of red currant or red raspberry jelly into a saucepan. Add the juice of 2 or 3 oranges and ½ lemon. Heat over a low flame,

stirring constantly, until jelly dissolves. Remove from heat and stir in ½ tablespoon Colman's mustard (more if you like it very hot) dissolved in a little orange juice. Strain, then add some very fine julienne rind of orange. Refrigerate to thicken.
This sauce will keep about 3 months when refrigerated. It is excellent with hot ham, cold cuts, turkey, pâtés.

CURRY SAUCE

Melt 2 tablespoons butter in a saucepan. Add 4 large onions, chopped, and cook until lightly browned. Stir in one generous tablespoon curry powder (more if you like it very hot), 2 tablespoons flour and a little salt. Gradually add a good consommé and simmer at least 15 minutes. Strain and add cream to taste.

DILL SAUCE

Make a Velouté (page 28) with chicken consommé. Add a little dry white wine, lots of finely chopped, fresh dill (or powdered), some grated onion, salt and pepper. Finish off the sauce with egg yolk mixed with cream. Serve with fish, seafood, or crayfish.

GAME SAUCE

Blend Basic Brown Sauce (page 10) with plenty of freshly ground black pepper, and a small amount of red currant jelly. Heat until jelly has melted, then stir in a little lemon juice and some flaming cognac—enough to please your taste. Work through a strainer and stir in a little cream. Should the sauce seem too thin, stir in a few pieces of Beurre Manié (page 10) and/or raw egg yolk, and heat. This sauce is served with game, turkey, and guinea hen.

GREEN SAUCE

Combine finely chopped, hard-cooked eggs, finely chopped watercress, parsley, tarragon and chives with Mayonnaise (page 15), a dash Worcestershire sauce, a touch of prepared mustard, and a few drops green food coloring (optional).

HERB SAUCE

This light sauce can be used, hot or cold, in place of mayonnaise. Beat together 3 egg yolks, salt and pepper, ½ cup milk, ½ cup strong consommé and the juice of ½ lemon. In the top of a double boiler melt ½ tablespoon butter. Stir in 1½ tablespoons flour as smoothly as possible. Pour in egg-yolk mixture, place over boiling water, and cook, beating constantly with a wire whisk, until smooth and thick. Add chopped herbs and a little cream, if you wish.

COLD HORSERADISH SAUCE

Combine ¼ cup grated horseradish with ¼ cup confectioners' sugar, a pinch of salt, 1 tablespoon vinegar, and 3 tablespoons whipped cream. Mix together thoroughly.

HOT HORSERADISH SAUCE

Combine ¼ cup grated horseradish with ¼ cup confectioners' sugar, a pinch of salt, 2 tablespoons fine bread crumbs, 2 tablespoons finely chopped almonds, 1 teaspoon or more vinegar, and 1 cup cream. Mix well and heat.

ITALIAN SAUCE

Poach a calves brain and remove all skin. Press through a sieve and mix with salt and pepper, prepared mustard, vinegar, chopped capers, tarragon, parsley, and oil.
Excellent with calf's head, cold cuts, and hot boiled beef. To be served cold.

MADEIRA SAUCE

Take some Basic Brown Sauce (page 10), bring to a boil with some fresh tomatoes, sliced, or canned tomatoes, drained. Add salt, pepper, and Madeira wine to taste. Strain. Thicken, if necessary, with Beurre Manié (page 10).

MINT SAUCE

Combine about 1 cup very finely chopped mint leaves with 2 tablespoons confectioners' sugar, 4 tablespoons cold consommé, a pinch of salt, and enough vinegar to please your taste.

sauces and basic preparations

SAUCE MORNAY

Make a Velouté (page 28) with mushroom stock or consommé, add plenty of chopped onion, salt, pepper, some grated Gruyère and Parmesan cheese. Strain, stir in an egg yolk mixed with cream, and add a little butter. Beat vigorously. This sauce is usually used on gratin dishes.

MUSTARD SAUCE

Make a thin Velouté (page 28) with fish stock or chicken consommé. Stir in ample French mustard, salt and pepper, egg yolk mixed with a little cream. Heat together, stirring constantly. Strain and serve with broiled or fried fish.

RASPBERRY OR STRAWBERRY SAUCE

Wash and drain fresh raspberries or hulled strawberries. Blend in an electric blender, then combine the purée with a little sugar. Cook over a low heat for about 10 minutes. Chill in refrigerator before serving over ice cream, pudding, peach or pear Melba. Sauce will keep under refrigeration for about 10 days.

STEAK SAUCE

Blend together 1 cup Basic Brown Sauce (page 10), dash sherry, 1 teaspoon butter, a little tomato purée, some grated onion, Worcestershire sauce, French mustard and heat over a low fire. If you prefer a thicker sauce, drop in a few small pieces of Beurre Manié (page 10). Stir with a wire whisk until mixture thickens.

TARRAGON SAUCE

Combine some Basic Brown Sauce (page 10) with a little consommé, plenty of tarragon leaves and a dash of dry white wine. Cook slowly until liquid has reduced to half the original amount. Stir in more basic brown sauce, strain, and add fresh tarragon leaves, coarsely chopped. Taste for salt and pepper.

TARTAR SAUCE

Mix finely chopped, hard-boiled eggs, a dash of prepared mustard, Worcestershire sauce, finely chopped dill pickle, and chopped parsley with Mayonnaise (page 15). Optional: a dash of sugar.

TOMATO SAUCE

Slice 6 large ripe tomatoes and cook with some consommé for about 20 minutes. Stir in a little tomato purée, some grated onion, salt and pepper, and cook to a boil again. Strain, thicken with a little Beurre Manié (page 10) and/or cream.

SAUCE VANILLE

Heat together 1 cup cream, 1 cup milk and 1 vanilla bean for about 5 minutes. Beat 4 egg yolks with ½ cup sugar until mixture drops from your spoon like a ribbon. Gradually stir in the milk-cream combination and cook over boiling water, stirring constantly, until sauce thickens. Strain, if necessary, and cool. Before serving, stir in whipped cream.

SAUCE VINAIGRETTE

Mix 3 parts oil, 1 part vinegar with salt, pepper and French mustard. Add a few drops Worcestershire sauce, and chopped parsley.
To serve with cold vegetables, add chopped onion, chopped hard-boiled egg, and 1 slightly beaten raw egg yolk.

WHITE WINE SAUCE

Make a Velouté (page 28) with mushroom stock or fish stock or consommé. Add dry white wine to taste, a little chopped onion, salt and pepper. Strain, and add cream mixed with egg yolk, or mix into it a teaspoonful of Sabayon (page 18). Taste and add more seasonings, if needed.

FISH STOCK

Combine well-chopped fish bones and heads, sliced onions, several sprigs of parsley, half a lemon and enough cold water to almost cover. Cook for about 30 to 40 minutes over a moderate heat. Strain and keep the stock ready for use in your refrigerator. It can be stored satisfactorily for about 3 days, but if the stock is boiled for 5 minutes after the third day it will keep for another 3 days.
Use in appropriate sauces or as the liquid for poaching fish.

VELOUTÉ

Velouté is a basic sauce made with stock and equal amounts of butter and flour. The stock can be chicken, beef, mushroom, fish or veal, depending on the dish it is to accompany. This recipe makes 2 cups of thick Velouté which can be thinned, if necessary, with more stock, with wine, or with cream.
Melt 3 tablespoons butter, but do not brown. Stir in 3 tablespoons flour smoothly and add a little grated onion, salt and pepper. Cook a minute or so. Pour in 2 cups hot stock and cook, stirring constantly, until mixture comes to a boil. Reduce heat and simmer about 10 minutes to develop flavor. Work through a sieve.

hors d'oeuvre and cold buffet

The recipes in this section
are equally appropriate
for cocktail parties, cold summer
luncheons, snacks, garden parties,
surprise parties,

or as a first course for a luncheon or dinner. Many of the recipes may be prepared a day or two ahead of time. The mousses are suitable not only for serving in the conventional fashion, but also as a spread for any type of sandwiches. Care has been taken to include here only those foods which are convenient to handle, and easy to eat even at a stand-up occasion.

The importance of attractive and appealing presentation of these cold dishes cannot be overemphasized. Serve them on your finest china or your best silver. Be careful to achieve a good range of colors. Eye appeal is important, as is also a wide selection of types and textures of foods. Some of the salads are made with mayonnaise, others with vinaigrette. Eggs, poultry and sea food are suggested. Some of the dishes are bland, others very highly seasoned; some are crisp, others smooth. Many people mistakenly believe that cold turkey, ham, or roast beef is all that is required for a successful cold buffet. The greater the number of guests the greater should be the variety of dishes.

AVOCADO MARYLAND

Cut avocados in half and peel. Combine finely chopped tuna with a little chopped onion, parsley, celery, lightly-sautéed green and red peppers, and enough Mayonnaise (page 15) to hold mixture together. Pile into halves of avocados.

SUGGESTED WINE:
Rosé de Provence
Serve chilled

STUFFED AVOCADO

Cut avocado in half lengthwise and peel. Make some Special Cocktail Sauce (page 21), mix with cooked chicken meat or shrimp or crabmeat and spoon into avocado cavities.

SUGGESTED WINES:
White Tarn — Gaillac Perlé
White Burgundy — Puligny–Montrachet
Serve chilled

BRAINS VINAIGRETTE

Slice cooked and skinned calf's brains about ½ inch thick, cover with Vinaigrette Sauce (page 27), sprinkle with capers and top with thinly sliced raw onion rings.

SUGGESTED WINE:
White Alsatian — Traminer
Serve chilled

CANTALOUPE MARSEILLAISE

Cut top off cantaloupe, scoop out most of the meat and cut half of it into small dice (use up remaining half some other way). Turn cantaloupe upside down and allow it to drain for about ½ hour. Combine diced cantaloupe with cooked, diced lobster, crabmeat or shrimp or a mixture of all 3 and all the remaining ingredients. Mix

sauce ingredients together, combine with cantaloupe seafood mixture and spoon into cantaloupe shell. Replace top and serve very well chilled. One medium-size cantaloupe will serve 2 to 3. Substitute a large Spanish melon, if you like, increasing the filling proportionately. It should serve from 6 to 8, depending on the size.

FILLING:

2 cups cooked lobster, crabmeat, or shrimp
1 hard-boiled egg, sliced
1 small tomato, sliced
3 to 4 cooked mushrooms, sliced
Salt
Pepper
½ teaspoon chopped tarragon or dill
Parsley

SAUCE:

2 tablespoons mayonnaise
1½ tablespoons ketchup
½ tablespoon dry white wine
½ tablespoon consommé
Salt
Pepper
Lemon juice
Dash Tabasco
Dash Worcestershire
1 teaspoon French mustard
2 tablespoons light cream

SUGGESTED WINES:

White Rhône – Hermitage
Red Provence
Serve chilled

CHEESE CREAM PUFFS

Make cream puff dough (page 15), spoon into pastry bag, and "shoot" on a buttered baking tin in very small heaps. Paint with beaten egg and allow to stand for about 5 to 10 minutes before placing in a preheated 450°F oven. Leave the door slightly open, so that any steam can escape. When well browned, take out and cool. When cool make a small incision on the side of each puff, near the bottom, and extricate the soft paste inside.

Make a smooth filling by mixing Roquefort or Danish Blue cheese with butter, add some paprika and stuff some of this mixture into each puff.

Excellent for cocktail parties or buffets.

SUGGESTED WINES:
Red Rhône — Hermitage
Red Rhône — Tavel
Beaujolais
Serve red Rhône and Hermitage chilled

SACHER CHEESE

Mix together 3 packages (3-ounce size) cream cheese with a sprinkling of salt, lots of paprika, some caraway seed, French mustard, 3 slightly beaten egg yolks, 3 small tins of anchovy fillets, finely chopped, with their oil. Work with some softened butter until mixture is very smooth. Mold into a dome with spatula, place in center of a flat serving dish, surround with small mounds of chopped parsley, finely chopped hard-boiled egg whites, sieved hard-boiled yolks, caraway seed and paprika. All around the dome of the Sacher Cheese, decorate with filets of anchovy and halves of green olives. Suggested for a cold buffet and also to serve with drinks.

SUGGESTED WINES:
Red Hermitage
Red Rhône — Tavel
Beaujolais
Serve first two chilled

CHICKEN BREASTS VILLEROY

To serve 6, take 3 chicken breasts, place in boiling salted water and let simmer until cooked. Then skin, debone, and cut lengthwise in half. Cool and dry well. Cover bottom of each breast about ¼ inch thick with canned purée of *foie gras* or Mousse of Duck Bellevue (page 38). Refrigerate until set. Then cover the top of the chicken breasts and the sides with White Chaud-froid Sauce (page 20). Decorate on top with crossed tarragon leaves on thin slices of truffles. Refrigerate until needed.

SUGGESTED WINES:
White Rhine (Hock) — Riesling
White Bordeaux — Graves
White Burgundy — Pouilly-Fuissé
Serve chilled

THE DEVIL'S EYE

Cut rounds of white bread 1½ inch in diameter. Fry in butter. Cool. Place 1 large or 2 small raw oysters in center of each piece of fried bread and surround with caviar. Serve with lemon and pepper mill.

SUGGESTED WINES:
White Loire – Muscadet
White Loire – Pouilly-Fumé
White Loire – Sancerre
White Burgundy – Chablis
Serve chilled

hors d'oeuvre and cold buffet

EGGS WITH ANCHOVIES

Slice hard-boiled eggs in half, lengthwise, cover with Mayonnaise (page 15), place 1 or 2 anchovy filets on top. Serve on Russian Salad (page 52). Decorate with asparagus spears and/or sour pickles.

SUGGESTED WINES:
White Alsatian – Traminer
White Burgundy – Pouilly-Fuissé
Serve chilled

HAM ROLLS WITH ASPARAGUS

Roll thin slices of cooked ham or prosciutto or Westphalian ham around one or more cooked asparagus spears. The number depends on the thickness of the asparagus. Hold together with a toothpick.

SUGGESTED WINES:
White Loire – Pouilly-Fumé
White Loire – Sancerre
Serve chilled

LEEKS VINAIGRETTE

Take small young leeks, wash thoroughly and trim off most of the green tops. Cook in salted water until tender. Drain, cool and cover with a mild Vinaigrette Sauce (page 27).

No wines with this salad

MARINATED MUSHROOM ORIENTAL

Take ½ pound mushrooms; if very large, cut them once or twice, wash and sauté lightly in butter. Add some crushed bay leaves, 1 large onion grated, 1 tablespoon chopped parsley, a little thyme, 1 cup tomato juice, ½ cup Basic Brown Sauce (page 10), 1½ cups dry red wine, 2 tablespoons butter, salt and pepper. Let simmer in covered pan until almost all liquid has disappeared. Serve cold.

SUGGESTED WINES:
White Muscadet – Loire
White Burgundy – Pouilly-Fuissé
Serve chilled

MOUSSE OF DUCK BELLEVUE

This mousse can also be made with the white meat of chicken, pigeon, wild duck, pheasant, or other feathered game.
Wash duck livers preferably or chicken livers, cleaned of their greenish spots. Fry livers in ample butter with onions, sliced, until partially cooked. Add bay leaves and cognac; ignite. Pour in enough dry red wine to cover livers, place lid on top and simmer until livers are well done and most of the liquid has been cooked away.
Take the cooked breasts of chicken or the duck meat, discarding skin, all bones and gristle, and work meat twice through the finest blade of the meat grinder (the electric blender can be used, but the grinder is better) along with the livers and all the liquid that remains in the pan. Season the mixture to taste with salt and pepper. Mix in egg yolks and one part sherry to two parts port wine (enough to

please your taste). Cool. Fold in heavy cream, whipped, and place in a large bowl or mold and refrigerate until firm.

At this stage decorate with slices of truffles or black olives. Pour Aspic (page 8) over all, about half a finger thick on top, and refrigerate until firm. Serve with Cumberland Sauce (page 21) on the side.

This mousse is also attractive spooned into the shells of oranges or tangerines.

15 duck livers or 20 to 25 chicken livers
Butter
2 large onions, sliced
2 bay leaves
3 to 4 breasts of chicken, cooked, or the meat of 2 roasted ducks
Salt
Pepper
2 egg yolks
Dry sherry
2 tablespoons cognac
Dry red wine
Port wine
2 to 3 cups cream, whipped
Truffles or black olives
Aspic

SUGGESTED WINES:
White or Rosé d'Anjou — Loire
White Bordeaux — Barsac
White Bordeaux — Graves
Serve chilled

HAM MOUSSE

Take 2 pounds lean cooked ham, pass twice through meat grinder, using finest blade. Immediately add ½ cup consommé, 1 tablespoon Basic Brown Sauce (page 10), ¼ envelope unflavored gelatin, 2 to 3 cups whipped cream. Mix well. Taste for seasoning. Place in serving dish, and smooth top with spatula dipped in cold water. Refrigerate until firm. Decorate with halves of black olives, pour over aspic and replace in refrigerator until set. Serve with Cumberland Sauce (page 21).

2 pounds of lean cooked ham
½ cup consommé
1 tablespoon basic brown sauce
¼ envelope unflavored gelatin
2 to 3 cups whipped cream

SUGGESTED WINES:
White or Rosé d'Anjou – Loire
White Bordeaux – Barsac
White Bordeaux – Gaillat
Serve chilled

MOUSSE OF HERRING À LA RUSSE

Skin and debone 2 salt herring. Soak in sparkling water for a few hours. Drain, dry, and mix with the following, all finely chopped: Hard-boiled eggs, large stalk celery, pared apples, small sour pickles. Add enough Mayonnaise (page 15) to bind. Place in serving dish and decorate with sour pickles, cut into fans.

This mousse makes a delicious spread for sandwiches or for cocktail biscuits.

2 salt herring
Soda water
4 hard-cooked eggs
1 large stalk celery
2 apples
2 sour pickles
Mayonnaise

SUGGESTED WINES:
White Rhine (Hock) – Riesling
White Bordeaux – Graves
Serve chilled

MOUSSE OF SHRIMP

Take 1 pound cooked, shelled and cleaned shrimp, mix with 1 cup thick Sauce Américaine (page 18), 1 tablespoon melted Lobster Butter (page 14), salt and pepper. Add a dash of cognac. 2 raw egg yolks, 3 tablespoons melted Aspic (page 8). Blend in electric blender. Season to taste after having added a little more cognac. Mix well with 1 to 1½ cups whipped cream, spoon into a serving dish, smooth with a spatula dipped in cold water, and decorate with cooked shrimp, sliced in half, lengthwise. Pour melted aspic over the mousse and refrigerate until firm.

SUGGESTED WINES:
White Rhine (Hock) – Riesling
White Bordeaux – Graves
White Burgundy – Meursault
Serve chilled

MOUSSE OF TUNA AMIRAL

Work 3 tins (7-ounce size) tuna with its oil and 4 small tins anchovy filets, also with their oil, through the finest blade of your meat grinder or blend in electric blender. Mix thoroughly with 1¼ cups (2¼ sticks) butter softened. Place in serving dish, smooth surface with spatula dipped in cold water. Refrigerate until firm. Garnish with halves of green olives and cover with Aspic (page 8).

3 tins (7-ounce size) tuna	Green olives
4 small tins anchovy filets	Aspic
1¼ cups (2¼ sticks) butter	

No wine with this mousse

ONIONS NIÇOISE

Sauté small white onions lightly in a mixture of butter and sugar. Add onion slices, raisins, tomatoes, a little more sugar, vinegar, consommé, tomato juice and dry red wine to cover. Place lid on pan and let simmer until vegetables are soft and almost all the liquid is absorbed. Taste and season with salt and, if necessary, more sugar and vinegar. Serve cold.

60 small white onions	Sugar
¼ cup of butter	Vinegar
¼ cup of sugar	2 cups consommé
4 large onions, sliced	2 cups tomato juice
½ cup of raisins	2 cups dry red wine

5 large tomatoes, skinned and sliced

SUGGESTED WINE:
Red Rosé – Provence
Serve chilled

CURRY PINEAPPLE

Cut rind off fresh pineapple, slice (discard woody core), then cut into dice and combine with curried Mayonnaise (page 15).

Wine is not particularly recommended but a chilled White Alsatian – Gewürztraminer could be served with this dish.

PINEAPPLE TROPICAL

Take 1 large pineapple and slice off the top third, cut out all the fruit and dice about ⅓ of it. Leave shell and plumage intact. Turn shell upside down and allow to drain for about ½ hour. Fill with same mixture as in Cantaloupe Marseillaise (page 32), substituting diced pineapple for the cantaloupe. Reassemble pineapple and serve very cold.

SUGGESTED WINES:
White Rhine (Hock) – Traminer
White Bordeaux – Barsac
White Rhône – Hermitage
Red Provence
Red Rhône – Tavel

PORK PATÉ

The following recipe should yield about 12 thick slices of pâté.
Take the lean pork (the best cut would be the filet), cut out all fat and sinews and pass once through the meat grinder together with raw duck livers or chicken livers and ½ pound salt pork. Set aside.
In the meantime, prepare thin strips of cooked white chicken meat, about 4 inches long, or duck meat from the breast and the same amount of cooked ham, cut in strips. Roll a thin slice of bacon around each strip of meat. Having made about 8 of each of these strips marinate them in cognac. To the pork-liver mixture add salt, freshly ground pepper, chopped tarragon and thyme, 4 egg yolks, ⅓ cup port wine, ⅓ cup cognac and, if you wish, some chopped truffles. Taste for seasoning after having mixed very well.
Line bottom and sides of an oven-proof mold or baking dish (dish must be at least 5 inches high or higher) with slices of bacon, cover with a 1-inch layer of the ground pork mixture, place 3 or 4 of the meat strips on top, all going in one direction, and sprinkle with a few small cubes of salt pork. Add another layer of the ground pork mixture, more meat strips, and salt pork cubes, and repeat until all is used. Cover with bacon slices, toss in 2 or 3 bay leaves. Place a tight-

fitting cover on top. Now make a heavy paste of flour and water and seal the outside where the lid joins the mold to make container airtight.

Place mold in a pan of boiling water (water should reach two-thirds up on the mold) and bake in a preheated, 450° F to 500° F, oven for 45 minutes. Take out of the oven, remove cover, and turn pâté out on a platter. Discard bacon, blot up any liquid, and cool pâté completely. When cold, replace in original mold (cleaned, naturally) and cover with a thick layer of Aspic (page 8). Refrigerate until well chilled and firm. This pâté is good for about 2 weeks.

2 pounds lean pork
15 raw duck livers or 25 raw chicken livers
½ pound salt pork
1 large chicken breast, cooked, or the breast meat
 from a roast duck
4 thick slices ham, cooked
½ pound sliced bacon (about)
Cognac
Salt
Freshly ground pepper
Tarragon, chopped
Thyme, chopped
4 egg yolks
⅓ cup port wine
⅓ cup cognac
Truffles (optional)
2 or 3 bay leaves
Flour
Aspic

SUGGESTED WINES:
Vintage Port
Serve at room temperature
White Bordeaux – Sauterne
White Bordeaux – Graves
Serve chilled

PUNCH-BOWL

WINE PUNCH-BOWL:

Slice 2 lemons, add 6 ounces of caster sugar, 2 glasses of white wine. Let stand for an hour or more. Before serving add 2 bottles of white wine and 2 bottles of soda water and ice. (about 25 glasses) Leave 1 whole rind of lemon in container.

STRAWBERRY PUNCH:

Place 1 pound of fresh, cleaned strawberries together with 7 ounces of caster sugar in a large container. Add ½ glass of kirsch (or brandy) and let soak for several hours at room temperature. Before serving add 2 bottles of white wine, 1 bottle of soda water, 1 bottle of champagne and ice cubes. Serves about 30 glasses.

PINEAPPLE PUNCH:

Place in large container ½ peeled and sliced pineapple, 5 ounces of sugar, 2 glasses of white wine and let soak in normal temperature for 1 hour or more. Before serving add 2 bottles of white wine and 1 bottle of champagne (or soda water) and ice cubes. Serves about 25 glasses.

PEACH PUNCH-BOWL:

Peel and slice about ¾ pound of fresh peaches. Add 6 ounces of caster sugar, glass of kirsch (or brandy) and let soak for several hours at room temperature. Before serving add 2 bottles of well chilled white wine and 1 bottle of champagne and ice cubes. (optional, instead of white wine: *only* champagne). Serves about 25 glasses.

hors d'oeuvre and cold buffet

RATATOUILLE

Take equal amounts of the following vegetables: red and green peppers, cut in strips, sliced cucumbers, onion, tomatoes, egg plant, and zucchini. Cook in consommé, adding tomato purée, until all are tender and most of the liquid has evaporated. Season with salt and pepper. Cool, then add mild Vinaigrette Sauce (page 27) and serve cold as an hors d'oeuvre. Ratatouille can also be served hot with certain meat and chicken dishes as a vegetable. (If served as a vegetable omit vinaigrette).

SUGGESTED WINES:
White Clairette du Languedoc
White Rhône – Hermitage
Red Rosé – Provence
Serve chilled

CURRY RICE

Combine cooked rice and chopped almonds with Mayonnaise (page 15) into which curry powder dissolved in cream has been added.

Wine is not particularly recommended but a chilled White Alsatian – Gewürztraminer could be served with this dish.

RICE À LA GRECQUE

Mix cooked rice with chopped peanuts, sardines, skinned tomatoes, raisins, and enough light Mayonnaise (page 15) to hold mixture together.

SUGGESTED WINE:
White Burgundy – Pouilly-Fuissé
Serve chilled

BEET SALAD

Cook fresh beets in boiling water until tender. Remove skins and cut into slices, cover with a mild Vinaigrette Sauce (page 27), flavored with a little horseradish. Or follow same recipe using canned beets, drained.

No wine with this salad

CAULIFLOWER SALAD

Cook whole cauliflower in equal amounts of milk and water, seasoned with salt. When tender, drain and separate into small pieces. Cool. Cover with Mayonnaise (page 15) which contains a strong accent of French mustard.

No wine with this salad

CHICKEN SALAD DUCHESSE

Take some cooked or sautéed chicken, discard skin and cut meat into thin strips. Combine with thin orange slices, a few crushed nuts, a few tips of cooked asparagus, sliced mushrooms, peas, chopped raw celery and julienne-cut raw carrots. Mix with Mayonnaise (page 15), thinned with a little cream.

SUGGESTED WINES:
White Rhine (Hock) – Riesling
White Burgundy – Meursault
Serve chilled

hors d'oeuvre and cold buffet

CUCUMBER SALAD

Peel cucumber and cut into thin slices, place in a strainer, sprinkle with salt, and let stand for about 30 minutes. Press slices with back of a spoon, rinse in cold water and press again. Combine with a mixture of sour cream, a pinch of sugar, vinegar, a little salad oil, a few drops of Worcestershire sauce, pepper and chopped chives. (optional: pinch of sugar)

No wine with this salad

DANISH SALAD

For 6 persons take about 10 cooked and skinless frankfurters, cut in thin slices, also about 15 small red radishes sliced, and 1 medium-size fresh cucumber, sliced. Mix all together with chopped herbs and a light Vinaigrette Sauce (page 27).

SUGGESTED WINES:
White Clairette du Languedoc
Red Rosé – Provence
Serve chilled

FISH SALAD

Take some pieces of cooked, poached fish, add some diced tomatoes, skinned, chopped parsley, diced cooked potatoes, some raw diced cucumbers, diced sour pickles, and mix with Special Cocktail Sauce (page 21).

SUGGESTED WINES:
White Rhine (Hock) – Riesling
White Moselle – Piesporter
Serve chilled

ITALIAN SALAD

Combine cooked sliced potatoes with cooked peas, diced salt herring, small cucumber cubes, chopped anchovies, coarsely chopped sour pickles, cooked cauliflower, well-drained capers and enough Mayonnaise (page 15) to bind the salad together.

SUGGESTED WINES:
White Loire — Pouilly-Fumé
White Italian Soave
Serve chilled

LOBSTER SALAD

Slice cooked lobster meat, add some small dices of fresh pineapple, or fresh or tinned peaches, slices of hard-boiled egg, and mix all with Tartar Sauce (page 26).

SUGGESTED WINES:
White Rhine (Hock) — Riesling
White Burgundy — Meursault
Serve chilled

MEAT SALAD

Any leftover cooked meat, such as roast beef, pot roast, veal, ham, pork, or tongue can be used here.
Cut meat in small cubes, add cubes of cooked potatoes, thin slices

of sour pickles, raw onion rings and coarsely chopped tomatoes. Toss all in a light Vinaigrette Sauce (page 27).

SUGGESTED WINES:
White Clairette du Languedoc
Red Rosé – Provence
Serve chilled

SALAD NIÇOISE

Take some green and black olives, bits of tinned tuna, thin strips of green and red peppers and lettuce cut in julienne, diced cucumbers, fresh tomatoes quartered, and hard-boiled eggs quartered, a few anchovy filets, salt and pepper to taste. Mix all with oil and lemon juice.

SUGGESTED WINE:
White Tarn – Gaillac Perlé
Serve chilled

POTATO SALAD

Cut cooked and peeled potatoes into thin slices, combine with a little chopped onion, some chopped cooked ham, salt and pepper. Combine with Mayonnaise (page 15).

SUGGESTED WINES:
White Rhine (Hock) – Riesling
White Alsatian – Gewürztraminer
Serve chilled

ROOT CELERY SALAD

Peel root celery and cook in boiling salted water for just a few minutes, leaving celery practically raw. Cut in very fine julienne and mix with Mayonnaise (page 15).

No wine with this salad

RUSSIAN SALAD

Combine cooked peas with cooked and diced green beans, carrots, cauliflower, beets, potatoes, raw and diced cucumbers, celery, tomatoes, and diced sour pickles, in equal proportions (and more or less the size of a pea), with enough Mayonnaise (page 15) to hold salad together.

SUGGESTED WINES:
White Rosé — Hermitage
White Rosé — Tavel
White Burgundy — Chassagne-Montrachet
Serve chilled

SAUSAGE SALAD WITH CHEESE ALSACIENNE

Slice cooked frankfurters about ¼ inch thick. Add an equal amount of diced Gruyère or similar cheese, sprinkle with chopped parsley, and cover with Vinaigrette Sauce (page 27).

SUGGESTED WINE:
White Alsatian — Gewürztraminer

hors d'oeuvre and cold buffet

SHRIMP SALAD

Make some Special Cocktail Sauce (page 21), add sliced, hard-boiled eggs, asparagus tips, chopped celery and chives, sliced mush-rooms, sautéed lightly in butter, and cooked, cleaned shrimp.

SUGGESTED WINES:
White Loire — Pouilly-Fumé
White Burgundy — Meursault
Serve chilled

SPANISH SALAD

Cook tomatoes, onions, zucchini, cucumbers slightly and drain. Then cut in thin slices. Arrange in alternate layers in a flat salad dish and cover with a light Vinaigrette Sauce (page 27).

No wine with this salad

SWEET CORN SALAD

Drain a tin of niblets well, add finely chopped red and green peppers, combine with Mayonnaise (page 15) mixed with a little cream.

No wine with this salad

SALMON IN ASPIC

For 6 people take about 2 pounds salmon, preferably the tail piece, and poach in salt water with ½ lemon. When cooked, skin immediately, debone, and scrape off all the dark gray parts under the skin. Cool.

Take a round or square serving dish, pour a thin layer of melted Aspic (page 8) on the bottom. Chill in refrigerator until firm. Then arrange the salmon, which has been cut into 6 or 7 equal pieces, in the dish, decorate in between the pieces with hard-boiled eggs halved, quarters of tomatoes, sliced cucumbers. Then add to the cool and melted aspic some port wine and pour it over the salmon. The aspic should cover the salmon by about ¼ inch (the salmon pieces can be decorated with either sliced truffles or crossed tarragon leaves). Serve Green Sauce (page 23) on the side.

SUGGESTED WINES:
White Clairette du Languedoc
White Burgundy – Corton
White Burgundy – Vougeot
Red Rhône – Tavel
Serve chilled

hors d'oeuvre and cold buffet

COQUILLE OF SALMON

For 2 persons, take 2 cups poached salmon* meat, cut in small pieces, add a few cooked mushrooms, some capers, a little tarragon, mix with Mayonnaise (page 15), and fill into a shell or small individual salad dishes.

* Other poached fish can be used equally well.

SUGGESTED WINES:
White Burgundy – Pouilly-Fuissé
Rosé de Provence
Serve chilled

ROLLS OF SMOKED SALMON

Roll small pieces of thinly sliced smoked salmon around 2 or 3 asparagus spears and hold together with a toothpick. Sprinkle with some grated horseradish.

SUGGESTED WINE:
White Loire – Pouilly-Fumé
Serve chilled

TOAST ROUENNAISE

Fry slices of white bread in butter, spread a ¼-inch layer of Mousse of Duck Bellevue (page 38) on top, cover with thin coating of Basic

Brown Sauce (page 10) and sprinkle with chopped parsley and fine breadcrumbs. Place under broiler briefly. Serve hot.

SUGGESTED WINES:
White Bordeaux – Barsac
White Burgundy – Macon
Rosé de Provence
Serve chilled

STUFFED TOMATOES

Remove skins from ripe tomatoes, cut off tops and spoon out most of the center. Fill it with shrimp, crabmeat or chicken salad (page 48).

SUGGESTED WINES:
White Clairette du Languedoc
White Burgundy – Meursault
White Burgundy – Pouilly-Fuissé
Serve chilled

soups

CREAM OF ASPARAGUS

Make a Velouté (page 28) with asparagus juice and consommé. Add grated onion, salt and pepper, simmer for about 20 minutes and strain. Then add some spears of asparagus and for each 2 to 3 persons 1 egg yolk mixed with 1 or 2 tablespoons whipped cream.

PUREÉ OF CALF'S BRAIN

Poach in salted water 2 fresh calf's brains, then skin. Make a thin Velouté (page 28) with consommé, add calf's brains, and blend in electric blender. To the purée add a little lemon juice, pepper and salt, 3 cups cream mixed with 3 egg yolks. Reheat before serving, then add some chopped chives and parsley. Serves 6 people.
A similar soup can be made using 2 sweetbreads instead of the calf's brains.

CONSOMMÉ GERMINY

Wash ¼ pound sorrel leaves, cut leaves in strips, and cook in concentrated chicken consommé. Before serving stir in 1 cup cream mixed with 3 egg yolks, salt and pepper. Reheat, beating constantly. When consommé starts to thicken, add 2 tablespoons butter. Do not boil. This serves about 4 persons.

CONSOMMÉ OF LOBSTER

For 6 persons cook about 5 cups of strong chicken consommé, add 1 cup diced, cooked lobster meat, 1 cup Fish Stock (page 28), ½ glass dry white wine, whiff of garlic, salt and pepper, dill, caraway seed, and some raw, diced tomato meat. Let simmer 20 minutes or ½ hour and, just before serving, add to each cup 1 teaspoon fresh butter.

CREAM OF CHICKEN

Make a Velouté (page 28) with strong chicken consommé and/or mushroom stock. Dice some cooked chicken meat, sliced mushrooms, asparagus spears, salt and pepper and add 1 egg yolk mixed with cream for each person. Beat well into the soup and before serving, stir into each portion 1 tablespoon whipped cream.

CRÈME DU BARRY
(CREAM SOUP MADE WITH ARTICHOKES)

Make a Velouté (page 28) with chicken consommé. Boil artichokes in salted water to which ½ lemon has been added. When artichokes are cooked, scrape off the edible part of the leaves, add the cleaned artichoke hearts, and blend in the electric blender. Add this purée to the Velouté. Season, add cream mixed with egg yolk and reheat before serving.

FISH SOUP À LA BASQUE

Take 6 cups Fish Stock (page 28), add 3 cups consommé, a pinch saffron, a pinch dissolved curry powder, some finely chopped parsley, thyme, diced tomato meat, and simmer for about 15 minutes. Add shrimp, oysters, mussels, and some pieces of poached fish. Serve with bread croutons. Serves 6 to 8 people.

LENTIL SOUP

Cover 2 pounds lentils with half water and half consommé. Add 6 medium-size onions, sliced and a little salt. Bring to boil, then simmer 2 to 3 hours. Blend almost all, about 9/10ths, of the soup in the electric blender. Add remainder with whole lentils and frankfurter slices to the purée. Reheat before serving. If soup is too thick, add a little more consommé. Optional, a few drops of vinegar. Serves 6 to 8 persons.

CREAM OF LETTUCE

Shred the lettuce and place in saucepan with butter. Add consommé to cover and cook several minutes. Make a Velouté (page 28) with consommé, add the cooked lettuce, and blend in electric blender. Replace in saucepan, adding cream and egg yolk, salt, and pepper. Reheat, but do not boil.

BISQUE OF LOBSTER

For 4 to 5 portions make a Velouté (page 28) with 4 tablespoons of Lobster Butter (page 14) and 2 tablespoons of flour and fish stock. Add some grated onion, paprika, salt and pepper, a little cognac, some small pieces cooked lobster, dry white wine and cream mixed with egg yolk, allowing one yolk for each cup. Stir this mixture into the Velouté. Heat well, but do not boil.

MINESTRONE

Fry some diced bacon until almost crisp. Add chopped celery, some julienned carrots, sliced onions, sliced tomatoes, small potato cubes, and coarse shreds of cabbage. Pour in consommé and cook about 20 minutes. Add some dried beans (these should have been soaked beforehand according to package directions), green beans, peas, rice and spaghetti, a touch of chopped garlic, a pinch of dried basil and thyme, salt and pepper to taste. Let simmer for about 1 hour. Serve with grated Parmesan cheese on the side.

CREAM OF MUSHROOM

Cook in consommé 2 pounds mushrooms with ½ lemon. When tender take out the mushrooms and blend in electric blender. Then make a Velouté (page 28) with the mushroom stock, add the purée of mushrooms, also a little dry white wine, salt and pepper, cream mixed with egg yolks, and chopped parsley. Reheat before serving. Serves 6 to 8.

ONION SOUP

A good onion soup depends on a very strong consommé. For 6 persons take 6 to 10 large onions and slice them. Fry the onion rings in butter until slightly brown, then add 8 cups consommé and 3 more large onions, sliced. Simmer on a low flame for 1 hour, add salt and pepper, grated Parmesan and Gruyère cheese. Pour soup into individual casseroles. Place large croutons on top, sprinkle with Parmesan cheese and place under broiler.

BISQUE OF OYSTERS

Make a Velouté (page 28) from fish stock. Stir in oyster liquor, a good deal of grated onion, salt and pepper. Add raw oysters and simmer a few minutes. Before serving, add cream mixed with yolk of egg. Reheat (don't boil) and sprinkle with chopped chives. Adding some dry white wine is highly recommended.

CURRIED PURÉE OF PEAS

Make a purée from fresh peas (see Saint Germain, page 63), adding curry powder to the Velouté (page 28). Before serving, add some cooked spaghetti.

CREAM SOUP SAINT GERMAIN

Cook 6 cups fresh garden peas until tender together with 2 medium-size onions and parsley. Strain and blend in electric blender. Add 4 cups consommé. Make a Velouté (page 28) with consommé, add the purée of peas, stir, simmer 10 to 15 minutes, then add cream, salt and pepper to taste. Serve with fried, diced croutons or add a few frankfurter slices. Serves 6 to 8 persons.

VICHYSSOISE

Take 6 large leeks, discard the green part, clean well, and wash and chop roughly. Slice 2 to 3 large onions. Boil leeks and onions until tender in 5 cups consommé. Then add 1 medium-size peeled, raw potato cut in half, salt and pepper, 3 cups milk. Simmer 30 to 60 minutes. Then blend all in an electric blender. Cool the liquid purée. If it is too thick, add a little more consommé. Chill, and before serving, add sweet cream and chopped chives. Serves 6 to 8.

vegetables

Only the fancy kind of vegetable recipes are included in this chapter. The standard ways to prepare fresh and canned vegetables are easily available in any basic cookbook.

When it is the height of the season for a particular vegetable, use of the fresh vegetable rather than its frozen or canned counterpart is recommended. At other times of the year, however, this is not necessarily the case.

Overcooking is a common mistake in the preparation of vegetables. Close attention should be paid to the vegetables as they cook, so that they may be served while their color is bright and their texture firm.

PURÉE OF ARTICHOKE

Scrape off the edible part of the leaves and combine with the hearts, or bottoms, of the artichokes. Proceed as for Purée of Peas and Green String Beans (page 70).

GREEN BEANS À LA CRÈME

Clean beans and cook in salt water until tender. Drain. Make a very thin Velouté (page 28) with consommé, mix with cream, season to taste, add green beans, and reheat.

BROCCOLI AU GRATIN

Boil the broccoli in salted water and when tender, drain well on a clean cloth. Butter the bottom of an oven-proof serving dish, cover with a thin Sauce Mornay (page 25), place broccoli on top, and spoon Sauce Mornay over it. Sprinkle with cheese and a few drops of melted butter and place under the broiler.

PUREÉ OF BROCCOLI

Remove the leaves if any, and cook broccoli in salt water until tender. Drain well on a clean cloth so no liquid remains. Blend in an electric blender and then proceed as for Purée of Peas and Green String Beans (page 70).

vegetables

GREEN CABBAGE, GERMAN STYLE

Slice a medium-size green cabbage in thin strips, add 1 cup chopped onion, 1 cup chopped bacon. Mix well with salt and pepper to taste and 1 tablespoon caraway seeds.
Melt 2 to 3 tablespoons butter in a saucepan, add cabbage mixture and stir for about 10 minutes. Add ¼ cup vinegar or less, 1 to 2 tablespoons sugar, half consommé and half water to cover, place lid on top, bring to boil and simmer until tender. Add 1 cup dry white wine and boil for a few minutes before serving.

RED CABBAGE

Slice 1 raw red cabbage in julienne. Melt some butter in a heavy saucepan. When the butter is slightly brown add salt and sugar, then the cabbage and stir for about 10 minutes. Add a little vinegar, several raw, peeled, apples, sliced, and half consommé and water to cover. Place lid on top and simmer for 30 minutes. Then add some dry red wine and simmer, covered, until tender. Taste for seasonings: salt, sugar and/or vinegar.

CARROTS À LA CRÈME

Take some young carrots and clean, cut ½ inch thick and about 2 inches long. Place in saucepan with just enough water to cover, add salt, a pinch of sugar and a large piece of butter. When tender and liquid is nearly absorbed, add cream and reheat.

PURÉE OF CARROTS

Chop coarsely ½ pound scraped carrots, 1 peeled onion, 1 cleaned leek, ½ raw potato, peeled. Cook in salted water until tender. Drain and blend in an electric blender with a few tablespoons consommé. Mix into the purée a little fresh butter and cream and season to taste. Optional: a dash of sugar.

STUFFED CUCUMBERS

Peel cucumbers and cut into 3 or 4 even pieces. Scrape out seeds and some of the meat. Cook in salt water until half tender. Then fill with stuffing called for in Stuffed Tomatoes (page 72). Place in hot oven until piping hot and, if you wish, sprinkle with grated cheese.

DUMPLINGS, GERMAN STYLE

For 6 to 8 people, take about 3 pounds potatoes, cook until tender, then mash while still hot. Mix with 2 eggs, a generous ¾ cup flour, salt, nutmeg, and work all together thoroughly. Form this dough into finger-long thin croquettes, roll in flour. Then fry in half butter and half oil until well-browned, over low fire. Serve with any roasted or broiled beef.

EGGPLANT NIÇOISE

Cut eggplant in half lengthwise, fry in butter. When tender, scrape out the inner part, chop finely with parsley, chives, tomato meat, onion, salt and pepper, adding some bread crumbs. Fill the eggplant shell with this mixture. Sprinkle with grated cheese and a few drops of melted butter and set under broiler.

MUSHROOMS À LA CRÈME

Take 1 pound mushrooms, wash well and drain. Sauté lightly in butter for a few minutes, add 1 teaspoon lemon juice, and some consommé. In the meantime make 2 cups Velouté (page 28) with the juice from the mushrooms, add approximately 1½ cups fresh cream, the mushrooms and a little dry white wine. Simmer for 5 to 10 minutes, adding some chopped chives and parsley, salt and pepper. Serve with fried croutons.

GLAZED ONIONS

Take about 40 small white onions, as uniform in size as possible. Place in large saucepan with 3 tablespoons butter, 2 tablespoons sugar and give them a stir. Then add 1 cup consommé, about 1 cup Basic Brown Sauce (page 10) and salt to taste. Cover and simmer until onions are tender and a little liquid remains. Add more sugar, if necessary.

PURÉE OF ONIONS

Place peeled, sliced onions in saucepan with butter, add consommé to cover, place lid on pan, and cook until tender. Then drain, blend in the electric blender, mix with thick Velouté (page 28) made with consommé, adding cream, salt and pepper to taste. Reheat.

PEAS, FRENCH STYLE

Take some small white onions, of uniform size, and cook in consommé until almost tender. Add some finely diced bacon or ham, chopped parsley and lettuce cut julienne, some very small sweet peas, and dash of sugar. Sprinkle lightly with flour and let simmer until vegetables are tender.

PURÉE OF PEAS AND GREEN STRINGBEANS

Cook equal amounts of green beans and garden peas in salted water until tender (always cook all green vegetables very slowly without a lid). Drain well, turn in melted butter, then blend in an electric blender. Stir in a dash of sugar. Taste for seasoning. Then mix in a small portion of fluffy whipped potatoes. If the purée does not seem light and fluffy, fold in some stiffly beaten egg whites. Reheat before serving.

vegetables

POMMES DAUPHINES
(CREAM PUFF DOUGH WITH MASHED POTATOES)

Make Cream Puff Paste (page 15). Mix an equal amount of this dough with the same amount of mashed potatoes. Form into little balls with 2 coffee spoons, dipped in water, or place in a pastry bag and push the dough out through a large tube, cutting it off in 2-inch lengths. Fry in deep fat until golden.

GRATIN OF POTATOES

Peel 10 medium-size potatoes, slice them about ⅛ of an inch thick, sprinkle with salt and pepper. Take a large oven-proof dish, rub the bottom slightly with garlic, then cover with melted butter, place the potatoes on top in layers.
Beat together 2 eggs and 2 cups cream. Pour mixture over the potatoes, sprinkle with Parmesan cheese and bake in pre-heated 300° F oven until slightly brown on top. This should serve about 6 people.

MASHED POTATOES AU GRATIN

Make some fluffy, whipped potatoes, place in buttered, oven-proof dish, mold attractively with spatula, sprinkle lavishly with Parmesan cheese, some melted butter, and brown well under broiler.

RATATOUILLE

(See page 47)

SPINACH AU GRATIN

Cook some fresh spinach leaves and drain well. Also cook some mushrooms, drain well, and slice thickly. Place the spinach leaves on the bottom of an oven-proof, buttered platter, cover well with sliced mushrooms, season with salt and pepper. Cover the sliced mushrooms with Sauce Mornay (page 25), sprinkle with cheese and place under the broiler to brown.

BRUSSELS SPROUTS MORNAY

Clean sprouts and cook in salt water until tender, drain well. Take an oven-proof, buttered dish, cover bottom with a thin layer of Sauce Mornay (page 25), place the sprouts on top and cover with sauce Mornay. Sprinkle with cheese and set under broiler to brown.

STUFFED TOMATOES

Take medium-size, ripe tomatoes, cut off tops, and scrape out seeds. Take some leftover cooked chicken or ham and chop fine, add salt and pepper, bind with a little Velouté (page 28), fill tomatoes with this mixture, sprinkle with bread crumbs, dot with butter, and bake in hot oven.

egg dishes

For breakfast, lunch, brunch, or late at night as a snack before going to bed, egg dishes are ideal. They are suitable for practically any occasion except for dinner. Essential to the success of all egg dishes is the use of very fresh eggs. If you have any doubts about the freshness of an egg, you may subject it to the following test: Add

½ ounce of salt to a quart of tepid water. Place an egg in the salted water. An egg which is less than one day old will stay on the bottom, an egg which is two days old will rise with the thick side up, an egg which is five days old will float, and is likely to have an unpleasant after-taste.
The recipes in this chapter include those for poached eggs, mollet eggs (eggs which are boiled in the shell and later peeled), scrambled eggs, fried eggs, omelets, and cocotte eggs. Feel free to experiment with the egg recipes. The special ingredients recommended here for use in a particular omelet recipe, for example, are often appropriate for eggs prepared in another fashion. Some of these egg recipes provide especially attractive and original ways to utilize quantities of leftovers.

EGGS COCOTTE À L'AMÉRICAINE

Butter individual cocotte dishes with Lobster Butter (page 14). On bottom of dishes place cooked, diced lobster. Break an egg over the lobster and cover to the brim of the dish with thin Sauce Américaine (page 18). Set dishes in a pan with simmering water and bake in an oven for about 10 minutes or until eggs have set.

OMELETTE WITH ASPARAGUS

Heat some asparagus spears. Make omelette, place ½ of warmed asparagus on omelette, then fold over omelette and top with remaining asparagus.

EGGS BRAGANZA

For each person, take 1 large tomato and cook, whole, until tender. Cut off top ⅓ of each tomato, scoop out most of the center, place a soft poached egg into the hollow, cover with Sauce Béarnaise (page 19).

OMELETTE CARDINAL (EGGS WITH SEAFOOD)

Dice some cooked lobster or crabmeat and mix with creamed Sauce Américaine (page 18). Make up the omelette, pour the heated sauce over, and sprinkle with parsley.

EGGS COCOTTE À LA CRÈME

Butter individual cocotte dishes. Sprinkle chopped ham on the bottom. Break an egg on top of the ham, sprinkle with salt and pepper. Add enough cream to fill the dish, shower with grated cheese and top with a few drops of melted butter. Place in a pan with enough simmering water to reach half way up the cocotte dishes. Bake in a preheated 350° F oven until eggs are set. If necessary, slide under the broiler to brown surface slightly.

CURRIED EGGS WITH SHRIMP TAHITI

Cook rice in boiling water to which a little curry powder has been added. When rice is tender and dry, press in individual buttered molds. Keep warm while you make the Curry Sauce (page 22). Add some cooked shrimp to the sauce. Boil eggs (1 for each mold) for 4 minutes, then remove shells. Turn rice out onto a serving dish, place an egg on top and cover with the shrimp curry sauce.

OMELETTE CHASSEUR
(EGGS WITH CHICKEN LIVERS AND MUSHROOMS)

For 4 persons, wash 12 chicken livers and pat dry. Cut into slices. Combine with 1 generous cup sliced mushrooms, fry in butter with coarsely chopped onion. When chicken livers are half done, stir in ½ cup dry red wine and ¼ cup Basic Brown Sauce (page 10). Simmer until livers are well done. Season with salt and pepper. Make up the omelette and spoon the chicken liver mixture either onto the omelette before folding, or the mixture can be served on top of the omelette after folding. In either event, sprinkle with chopped parlsey before serving.

SCRAMBLED EGGS WITH CHEESE

Prepare scrambled eggs as described in Eggs Dieppoise (page 78). While the eggs are cooking, little by little stir in half grated Parmesan, half Gruyère cheese, adding enough to please your taste. Season with salt and pepper.

SCRAMBLED EGGS DIEPPOISE (EGGS WITH SEAFOOD)

Beast 5 eggs well, stir in a pinch nutmeg, chopped chives and dill, salt and pepper. Melt 4 tablespoons butter in a skillet. When hot (but still without color) spoon about 1 tablespoon of the butter into the beaten eggs and stir. Now, pour eggs into skillet with the remaining butter and stir constantly over a very low flame, until eggs begin to form. Add another tablespoon butter. Continue stirring until the eggs have a light, very soft consistency. Finish off with some cooked shrimp and freshly ground pepper before serving.

COLD EGGS IN DILL SAUCE

Boil eggs 4 to 5 minutes, peel, and let cool. Make Herb Sauce (page 23) or Mayonnaise (page 15), adding an ample amount of chopped dill and parsley. Take individual cocotte dishes. Place on bottom some julienne-cut, cooked ham, top with cold cooked egg and fill dish with the dill sauce.

EGGS DUCHESSE (EGGS WITH ARTICHOKES)

Poach eggs. For each egg take a fairly large cooked artichoke bottom. Keep the eggs and the artichoke bottoms warm. Set eggs on top and cover with a fairly thick Tarragon Sauce (page 26).

egg dishes

EGGS COCOTTE DU BARRY (EGGS WITH CALF'S BRAIN)

Take individual buttered cocotte dishes and fill each about ⅓ with cooked purée of calf's brain, salted and peppered. Break egg on top and fill to the brim with Madeira Sauce (page 24). Set in pan with simmering water and place in oven until eggs are cooked.

POACHED EGGS FLORENTINE (EGGS WITH SPINACH)

Butter a shallow baking dish. Spoon a layer of cooked, well-drained and dried spinach leaves on the bottom. Place poached eggs (yolks should still be soft) on top of spinach. Make a Velouté (page 28) with consommé, stir in some cream and egg yolk and also a little grated cheese. Pour sauce (make sure it is not too thick) over the eggs. Sprinkle with more grated cheese and brown under the broiler.

POACHED EGGS FONTAINE

Poach eggs and keep warm. For each egg fry 1 round piece of white bread the same size as the egg, and spread with Mousse of Chicken Bellevue (page 38) or tinned purée of *foie gras*. Set the egg on top, then cover with a thin Sauce Mornay (page 25). Sprinkle with cheese and set under hot broiler to take on color.

COLD POACHED EGGS EN GELÉE

Poach eggs (or boil for 4 minutes, then remove shell) and set aside to cool. Cover bottom of individual cocotte dishes with a thin slice of ham. Place egg on top of the ham. Fill to the brim with Aspic (page 8) flavored with a little sherry or port wine. Decorate with leaves of fresh tarragon or a slice of truffle. Chill until aspic is firm.

SCRAMBLED EGGS HAMBOURGEOISE

For 4 persons take ½ pound smoked fish (spats), skin and debone, cut into small pieces. Then sauté lightly in butter, add 3 to 4 tablespoons Basic Brown Sauce (page 10) and keep warm. Make your scrambled eggs with 8 eggs. Place the fish with its sauce in the center of the serving dish and spoon the scrambled eggs all around.

EGGS MEYERBEER

Break eggs into a buttered flame-proof dish and fry over low heat. While eggs are frying, add small chunks of tomato and some cooked chicken livers, salt and pepper. Pour over the tomatoes and chicken livers some hot Basic Brown Sauce (page 10) to which a little dry red wine has been added. Serve hot.

OMELETTE MISTRAL

Skin 1 or 2 tomatoes, then chop coarsely and sauté several minutes. Add a little crushed garlic, some julienne of ham, tarragon leaves, chopped parsley, salt and pepper. Heat all together and keep warm. To cook omelette, beat 4 egg yolks. Then in a separate bowl beat 4 egg whites slightly. Combine the beaten egg whites with the beaten yolks, adding 2 tablespoons whipped cream. Cook omelette and when done, spoon tomato mixture on top. Fold over omelette and cover with a thin layer of whipped cream. Sprinkle with grated cheese and brown quickly under very hot broiler. Serves 2 to 3 persons.

OMELETTE WITH MUSHROOMS

Cook some mushrooms, bind with Velouté (page 28) made with mushroom stock. Add a little dry white wine, salt and pepper. Blend in the electric blender. Reheat. Make the omelette. When cooked, fill with mushroom mixture, having tasted for seasoning. Fold over the omelette and cover with a thin Sauce Mornay (page 25), sprinkle with grated cheese and place under the hot broiler to brown.

OYSTER OMELETTE

Make a Velouté (page 28) using juice from the oysters and some Fish Stock (page 28). Stir in a little dry white wine, chopped parsley and tarragon, and if sauce is too thick, add some cream. Add oysters and heat, but do not bring to a boil. Make the omelette and when cooked, serve the hot oyster sauce over it.

OMELETTE PAYSANNE

For 4 persons take 2 cups leftover meat such as roast beef, veal, tongue, ham, and cut in dice about ½ inch. Take about the same amount of cooked and diced potatoes, ½ cup thinly sliced onions, place in a skillet and brown well in butter. Season with salt and pepper.

In a second skillet place ample butter and pour in 7 or 8 slightly beaten eggs, add the meat and potatoes and cook slowly. When done, fold over and serve.

EGGS ROUENNAISE (EGGS WITH FOIE GRAS)

Butter some individual cocotte dishes. Place on bottom 1 tablespoon Mousse of Duck (page 38) or 1 tablespoon tinned purée de foie gras. Break an egg on top, then fill the cocottes with Madeira Sauce (page 24). Set dishes in a pan of simmering water and bake in a preheated 350° F oven until eggs are done. If necessary, add a little more well heated Madeira sauce before serving.

SCRAMBLED EGGS WITH TOMATOES

Skin some ripe tomatoes, chop coarsely, add chopped parsley and chives, season with salt and pepper, and sauté in a little oil. Prepare some scrambled eggs and serve with the tomatoes heaped in the center of the serving dish or mixed into the eggs.

egg dishes

SCRAMBLED EGGS WITH TONGUE

Take some smoked, boiled ox tongue and cut in julienne. Heat in Basic Brown Sauce (page 10), adding a few drops of Madeira wine. Place in the center of serving dish and spoon scrambled eggs all around the tongue.

FRIED EGGS À LA TURQUE

Butter heavily the bottom of some individual flame-proof dishes, add 1 tablespoon finely chopped onion to each dish. Break 2 eggs on top, sprinkle lavishly with Parmesan cheese. Set under hot broiler and when eggs are done pour a ribbon of tomato ketchup around the eggs.

OMELETTE VAUDOISE (EGGS WITH CHEESE)

For 3 persons break 6 eggs into a bowl, add ½ cup cream, about 5 tablespoons grated Gruyère cheese, chopped parsley, chives and tarragon, salt and pepper. Beat all together. Fry 4 slices lean bacon, diced, with a little butter. Add 2 tablespoons more of butter, then the egg-cheese mixture and finish the omelette.

SCRAMBLED EGGS WINDSOR (EGGS WITH CALF'S BRAIN)

This recipe can be made either in the kitchen or at the table in a chafing dish. Chop cooked, skinned calf's brain very fine and mix with chopped chives. Make some very fluffy scrambled eggs in a chafing dish (or a skillet in the kitchen), then stir in the chopped brains. Season with salt and pepper before serving.

small dishes

The recipes in this section
are for interesting and unusual foods
which may be used as the main dish
for a light luncheon, when preceded by
a soup course, and supplemented by an appropriate salad.

Or they may be used as the first course of a dinner party, in which case somewhat smaller individual servings are recommended. In many instances, these small dishes offer practical and delicious ways of using up leftovers. Thrifty housewives will find them appropriate for a simple family luncheon or a late evening snack.

HEARTS OF ARTICHOKE STRASSBOURGEOISE

Cook some large artichokes in water with ½ lemon and salt. Remove the leaves so that only the clean bottoms of the artichokes remain. Fill the bottoms with *foie gras,* (purée of *foie gras* may also be used), then cover with a thin Sauce Mornay (page 25), sprinkle with cheese, and place under the broiler to brown.

SUGGESTED WINES:
Red Bordeaux (Claret) – Médoc
Red Bordeaux (Claret) – Saint Emilion

STUFFED CABBAGE, BAVARIAN STYLE

Open the cabbage leaves a little without breaking them and steam the head until the leaves are pliant. Pull off leaves, cutting out the thick stems. Combine pork, beef, liver, onion, salt, pepper, parsley, the whole egg plus extra egg yolks and mix together thoroughly. Take a large cabbage leaf, spread some of the meat mixture over the surface, cover with another leaf, spread with more meat mixture. Repeat until you have 3 to 4 layers, then roll up like a diploma and

tie together with a thread. Make up as many rolls as you have ingredients.
Fry cabbage rolls in melted butter until brown on all sides. Add enough consommé to almost cover. Put lid on the pan and simmer gently for about 30 to 40 minutes. Remove threads before serving. Serve with rice and Tomato Sauce (page 26). Serves about 6.

1 very large green cabbage
1 pound lean ground pork
1 pound ground beef
2 slices calf's liver, ground
1 large onion, grated
Salt
Pepper
¼ cup chopped parsley
2 egg yolks
1 whole egg
¼ cup (½ stick) butter
Consommé

SUGGESTED WINES:
Red Rhône – Tavel
Red Beaujolais

CAMEMBERT À LA VIERGE

Take a small Camembert, not too ripe, or a similar creamed cheese, and slice in half, across. Leave the crust on the cheese. Sprinkle on all sides with a little sugar and paprika, turn in flour, then in beaten raw egg and then in bread crumbs. Fry quickly golden brown in butter and serve hot.

SUGGESTED WINES:
Red Bordeaux (Claret) – Médoc
Red Beaujolais

CANNELLONI WITH CHEESE AND SPINACH

Fill one part of cannelloni with a mixture of cream cheese and the other part with purée of spinach. Place in buttered baking dish, cover with thin Sauce Mornay (page 25), sprinkle lavishly with grated cheese, and broil golden brown.

SUGGESTED WINES:
White Moselle – Bernkastel
White Orvieto – Secco

CAULIFLOWER SOUFFLÉ

Cook a small white cauliflower in half milk and half water, salted. When tender, drain thoroughly and place in a buttered and bread-crumbed soufflé dish. Make a Béchamel Sauce (page 10) with 2 tablespoons butter, 2 tablespoons flour and hot milk (the Béchamel should be thick enough to fall in lumps from a spoon). Then add 2 tablespoons grated Parmesan cheese, a few drops lemon juice, grated onion, salt, and pepper. Simmer for a few minutes, take off the fire, and, while still hot, beat in 3 egg yolks. Cool slightly. Then fold in 3 stiffly beaten egg whites. Pour mixture over cauliflower, sprinkle with grated cheese, a few drops of melted butter, and bake in a preheated 350° F to 400° F oven for about 30 minutes.

1 small cauliflower	Lemon juice
Milk	Grated onion
Butter	Salt

Bread crumbs
Flour
Parmesan cheese, grated
Pepper
3 eggs

SUGGESTED WINES:
White Rhine (Hock) – Riesling
Red Rhône – Châteauneuf-du-Pape

CRÊPES VILLEROY

Make large, very thin Crêpes (page 11) and keep warm. Chop left-over chicken meat with parsley, add sliced, cooked mushrooms, mix with White Wine Sauce (page 27), and spoon some of the chicken mixture on each crêpe. Fold crêpe over and place in a shallow, lightly buttered baking dish. Cover with more of the white wine sauce, thinned with a little cream, sprinkle with grated Gruyère cheese and brown slightly under hot broiler.

SUGGESTED WINES:
White Rhine (Hock) – Rüdesheimer
White Swiss – Neuchâtel

CHEESE SOUFFLÉ MIMOSA

For 2 persons take a soufflé mold 4½ inches in diameter and 2½ inches high. Prepare the mold with butter and fine bread crumbs. Melt 2 tablespoons butter adding, bit by bit, as much flour as the butter will absorb. Then add, also bit by bit while beating constantly, enough hot milk to make a thick Béchamel. Season with salt and pepper. Simmer, then add a little grated onion, 2 or 3 tablespoons Gruyère cheese, grated, ½ teaspoon Colman's mustard. Cool thoroughly. Then stir in 3 egg yolks well, finally fold in 3 stiffly beaten egg whites. Pour into the prepared soufflé dish, sprinkle with bread crumbs and a little melted butter or arrange several triangles of Gruyère, sliced paper thin, on top of mixture. Place briefly under a very hot broiler until a slight skin forms on top, then into a preheated 400°F to 450°F oven for 5 minutes. Reduce oven heat to 300°F or 350°F and continue cooking until soufflé is done.

Butter	Pepper
Bread crumbs	Grated onion
Flour	Gruyère cheese
Milk	Colman's mustard
Salt	3 eggs

NOTE: Cooked peas and/or diced cooked ham or meat or lobster or crab can be added to the mixture.

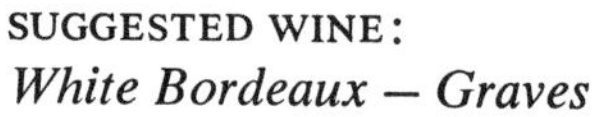
SUGGESTED WINE:
White Bordeaux – Graves

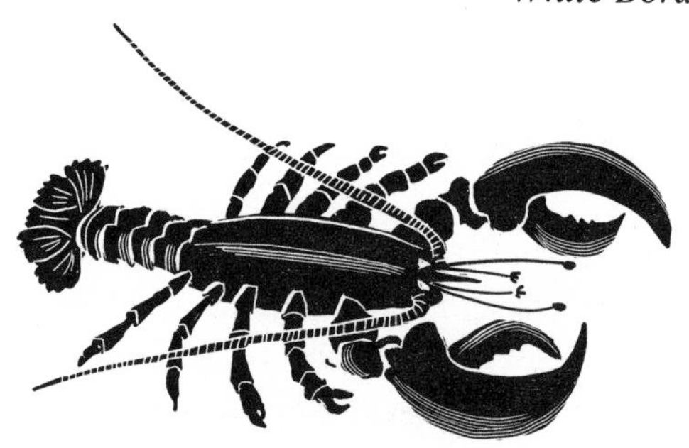

SOUFFLÉ OF LOBSTER BEATRICE

For a soufflé for 2 people take 1 heaping tablespoon Lobster Butter (page 14) and 1 tablespoon flour and make a Velouté (page 28) with fish stock. Add a little cognac, paprika, salt, and pepper. See to it the consistency is thick. Take 4 tablespoons of this Velouté, cool slightly, and beat in 4 egg yolks. Add ½ cup lobster meat, cut in small pieces, and mix well. Then fold in stiffly beaten egg whites (beaten to the dry stage). Spoon immediately into soufflé dish which has previously been coated lightly with lobster butter and fine bread crumbs. Sprinkle top of mixture with melted lobster butter and place under a very hot broiler until a slight skin has formed on top. Place in a preheated 400°F oven for about 8 to 10 minutes, then reduce heat to about 300°F and bake until done.

1 tablespoon Lobster Butter
1 tablespoon flour
Fish stock
Cognac
Paprika
Salt
Pepper
4 egg yolks
½ cup Lobster Meat
4 or 5 egg whites
Bread crumbs

SAUCE: Take remaining Velouté and mix in a little lobster butter, a few more drops cognac, ½ cup cream mixed with 1 egg yolk. Reheat, but do not boil.

SUGGESTED WINES:
White Burgundy — Meursault
White Burgundy — Pouilly-Fuissé

MUSHROOM PUDDING

Take 1 pound whole mushrooms, sauté in butter with 1 tablespoon grated onion, adding a little dry white wine. Then make a thick Velouté (page 28) with mushroom liquid (or consommé) (2 tablespoons flour to 2 tablespoons butter). To the Velouté add cream, egg yolks, salt, pepper, chopped parsley, and blend in an electric blender with the mushrooms. Fold into this purée, 6 stiffly beaten egg whites. Spoon into buttered soufflé dish. Place in a pan with simmering water and bake in a preheated 400° F oven for 45 minutes. See to it the water is constantly simmering, adding more boiling water if it evaporates.

1 pound mushrooms
Butter
1 tablespoon grated onion
Dry white wine
Mushroom liquid or consommé
2 tablespoons flour
2 tablespoons butter
½ cup cream
3 egg yolks
Salt
Pepper
Parsley, chopped
6 egg whites, stiffly beaten

SUGGESTED WINES:
White Loire — Pouilly-Fumé
White Burgundy — Clos de Vougeot
White Burgundy — Pouilly-Fuissé

ONION TART LYONNAISE

Coat a spring mold with butter and flour (the mold should be about 10 to 12 inches in diameter). Make a dough Brisée (page 16) with half the quantities given in the recipe, leaving out the sugar, but adding a pinch of salt.
Slice about 1 pound onions thinly, place them in a saucepan with melted butter, add a little consommé and sugar. Place lid on top and simmer over a very low flame until tender. Beat in a bowl 4 eggs, ½ cup milk, ¾ cup cream, 5 tablespoons grated cheese, salt, and pepper. Press dough into spring mold about ⅛ of an inch thick and spread onions on bottom. Pour egg-cheese mixture on top and bake in a preheated 350° F oven for approximately 30 minutes.

SUGGESTED WINES:
White Moselle – Bernkastel
White Loire – Pouilly-Fumé

BARQUETTE ORIENTALE

Bake for each person 1 or 2 Barquettes (page 9) and for each portion take 1 skinned, deboned sardine, chopped, a heaping ½ tablespoon Camembert cheese, a little French mustard, 2 anchovy fillets, and ¼ of a raw apple chopped. Pile this mixture into the barquette. Sprinkle with paprika and serve cold.

SUGGESTED WINES:
White Alsatian – Gewürztraminer
White Loire – Pouilly-Fumé

DEVILLED OYSTERS

Combine some cubes of Dutch or Cheddar cheese with a little butter, a small amount of finely chopped Chorizo sausage and add paprika. Heat, stirring constantly, until the cheese melts. Add some Worcestershire sauce and a few drops of Tabasco sauce to taste. If too thick, add a little cream. Cover the oysters (see Oysters Mornay (page 95) for sauce) and set under hot broiler until golden brown.

SUGGESTED WINES:
White Burgundy – Chablis
White Burgundy – Pouilly-Fuissé

OYSTERS HAMBOURGEOISE

Remove large oysters froms their shells, wash and dry shells. Pepper the oysters, dip in flour, then in lightly beaten egg, toss in bread crumbs, and fry in heated oil until crisp and brown. Spoon a little warm sauerkraut in each oyster shell, place a fried oyster on top and sprinkle with horseradish.

SUGGESTED WINES:
White Loire – Pouilly-Fumé
White Burgundy – Chablis

OYSTERS MEUNIÈRE

Take some medium-size oysters out of their shells and reserve the juice. Clean the shells. To the oyster juice add pepper, lemon juice, finely chopped onion and parsley. Put the oysters back into the shells and pour some of the mixture over each oyster, sprinkle with bread crumbs, dot with butter, and set under hot broiler until the oysters start to curl.

SUGGESTED WINES:
White Rhine (Hock) – Riesling
White Alsatian – Gewürztraminer

OYSTERS MORNAY

Take fresh oysters out of their shells, wash and dry the shells, replace the oysters, cover with thin Sauce Mornay (page 25), and broil until golden brown.

SUGGESTED WINES:
White Rhine (Hock) – Riesling
White Moselle – Bernkastel

OYSTERS À LA PAULETTE

For 3 persons take 30 small to medium-size oysters, and take them out of their shell. Reserve the liquor, make a Velouté (page 28) with fish stock and the oyster juice (2 cups of Velouté will be sufficient), add ½ cup dry white wine, 2 tablespoons chopped onion, some chopped parsley and boil for about 5 minutes. Then add oysters, and let simmer until edges begin to curl. Add 4 to 5 tablespoons Sabayon (page 18) and 1 cup cream. Reheat, but do not boil. Serve

in soup plates. Instead of the sabayon, one can add to the 1 cup of cream 3 egg yolks and 1 additional tablespoon of dry white wine. This dish can either serve as a first course for lunch or as a main course.
Instead of the oysters, this dish can be made with mussels in their shells.

SUGGESTED WINES:
White Moselle – Bernkastel
White Alsatian – Traminer

SOUFFLÉ OF OYSTERS

This recipe for 2 to 3 persons is adequate for a soufflé mold of about 6 inches in diameter by about 2½-inches high.
Butter the mold and coat lightly with fine bread crumbs. Take 16 medium-size oysters, dry well, reserve oyster juice, chop the oysters. Make a Velouté (page 28) with half-oyster juice, half-milk, salt and pepper, nutmeg. Cool. Beat 5 or 6 egg yolks into the heavy Velouté. Add 1 tablespoon dry white wine, the chopped oysters, then fold in 5 or 6 stiffly beaten egg whites (the whites of eggs should be beaten until practically dry). Spoon into prepared dish. The mixture should come to within ½ inch of the rim of the mold. Place under very hot broiler for 1 minute or 2 until a skin forms on top. Place in a preheated 400° F oven. After about 3 minutes reduce to 300° F and cook until the soufflé is done.
The baking time depends greatly on the size of the mold. For instance, if you take a mold of 4 inches in diameter by 2¼ inches high, which is ample for 1 person, the baking time will be about 12 to 15

minutes. The Velouté should be measured by 2 well-heaped tablespoons and 2 egg yolks per person. If you make a soufflé for more than 3 people, you can use 1 egg yolk and 1 tablespoon Velouté less. Making a soufflé in one mold for more than 5 to 6 persons is not recommended. Remember the old saying: "The soufflé doesn't wait for your guests, the guests must wait for the soufflé."

Butter
Bread crumbs
16 medium-sized oysters
6 tablespoons Velouté
Pepper
Salt
Nutmeg
5 or 6 egg yolks
5 or 6 whites of eggs
1 tablespoon white wine

SUGGESTED WINES:
White Rhine (Hock) – Rüdesheimer
White Alsatian – Traminer
White Burgundy – Chablis

POTATOES STRASBOURGEOISE

Take some boiled, peeled, sliced potatoes, mix with diced salt herring, add some cream mixed with raw egg yolk, pour over the potatoes, sprinkle generously with grated cheese and bake in the oven. Whenever using salt herring, it is advisable, after skinning and deboning, to soak the filets for a few hours in sparkling water before using.

SUGGESTED WINES:
White Alsatian – Traminer
White Swiss – Neuchâtel

RISOTTO MILANAISE

To serve 3 persons cook 1 cup of rice in a mixture of half consommé and half Basic Brown Sauce (page 10). When rice is tender and dry, combine with sautéed chicken livers, cooked peas, and grated cheese. Press into individual buttered molds, turn out, and sprinkle with more grated cheese before serving.

SUGGESTED WINES:
White Rhine (Hock) – Deidesheim
White – Soave

COQUILLE OF SALMON MORNAY

Mix pieces of poached salmon (or any other delicate fish) with sliced cooked mushrooms and shrimp, take some scallop shells (or individual cocotte molds), coat lightly with butter, fill with the fish, cover with Sauce Mornay (page 25) which should not be too thick but, on the other hand, should coat surface handsomely. Sprinkle with cheese, dot with a little butter, and broil until golden brown.

SUGGESTED WINES:
White Burgundy – Chablis
White Burgundy – Clos des Mouches
White Burgundy – Montrachet

BARQUETTE OF SARDINES

Bake some Barquettes (page 9). Skin and debone tinned sardines and chop together with an equal amount of fresh tomato meat. Bind with a little Velouté (page 28) made with a thin Sauce Mornay (page 25), sprinkle with Parmesan cheese and set under broiler to brown.

SUGGESTED WINES:
White – Soave
Red Rhône – Tavel

SARDINES AU GRATIN À LA TURQUE

Take a fireproof dish and rub bottom with crushed garlic, then cover with a little oil. Peel and slice tomatoes, and place half of them on bottom of baking dish. Cover and place in a preheated oven. When the tomatoes are cooked, remove them from oven and place 8 to 10 large skinned, canned sardines on top of tomatoes. Cover these with the remaining sliced tomatoes, sprinkle with fine bread crumbs, a few drops of oil, salt and pepper, and grated cheese. Set under the broiler to gratiner for about 10 minutes.

Garlic
Oil
6 large tomatoes
8 to 10 sardines
Bread crumbs
Salt
Pepper
Grated cheese

SUGGESTED WINE:
Red Rhône – Tavel

SPAETZLE

Combine in a bowl 4 cups all-purpose flour, a pinch of salt, and 3 eggs. Work the mixture with your hands thoroughly. Add 1 cup cold water, bit by bit, beating hard until dough develops blisters. Set aside to rest for about 1 hour. Place on a board and scrape dough off in small strips into a pan of boiling salted water. As soon as the spaetzle starts swimming on top, lift out with a slotted spoon. Before serving turn in melted butter. Spaetzle can be served as a first course with grated cheese or as a substitute for potatoes or rice with stews or roasts. They are also very tasty if, after poaching, they are browned in butter.

BARQUETTE SAINT MARTIN

For 6 persons bake 6 to 8 Barquettes (page 9). Chop roughly 1½ cups cooked crabmeat together with ½ cup raw tomato meat and ½ cup melon meat. Add ½ teaspoon grated onion, a little tarragon, and bind mixture with Curry Mayonnaise (page 15). Spoon into barquettes. Decorate with halves of black olives and serve cold.

SUGGESTED WINES:
White Rhine (Hock) – Rüdesheimer
White Bordeaux – Graves

STEAK TARTARE

For each portion take about ½ pound lean filet of beef. Chop more or less finely and mix with salt and freshly ground black pepper. In a bowl mix 1 egg yolk, 1 teaspoon French mustard, a few drops oil (lemon juice, ketchup, and 1 raw egg yolk; grated horseradish optional), chopped parsley and onion, drained capers, Worcestershire sauce, and mix all together thoroughly with the meat. Then form with 2 spoons to the shape of a filet mignon. Sometimes steak Tartare is served with a raw yolk and paprika on top.

SUGGESTED WINES:
Red Bordeaux (Claret) – Saint Emilion
Red Burgundy – Côte de Nuits

TIMBALE CASIMIR

Cook some rice and press into a buttered mold. Keep hot while you prepare the following: Combine diced cooked chicken meat, diced cooked ham, poached fish, cooked shrimp and oysters, raisins, olives, cooked mushrooms, sliced almonds. Make a Curry Sauce (page 22) and stir in all the ingredients. Heat well and serve around the molded rice.

SUGGESTED WINES:
White Burgundy – Chablis
White Burgundy – Meursault

TIMBALE JEANNETTE (A MOLD OF CALF'S BRAINS OR SWEETBREADS, EGGS, AND CHEESE)

For 5 to 7 people, make a thick Béchamel Sauce (page 10). Reserve 5 tablespoons and put aside to use later on. To the remaining Béchamel add 7 egg yolks, also salt, pepper, nutmeg, grated onion, and a large skinned, raw calf's brain which has been passed through a sieve. Fold 7 stiffly beaten egg whites and ½ cup cooked garden peas into the mixture. Butter a timbale or ring mold, sprinkle with fine bread crumbs, and spoon in the mixture. Set mold in simmering hot water, cover, and cook for 1 hour. Remove lid at this point, place mold in a preheated 450° F oven for 15 to 20 minutes. Turn out on warm serving platter. Serve at once.

FOR BECHAMEL:

½ cup (1 stick) butter
1 cup flour

TO MAKE THE SAUCE TO ACCOMPANY TIMBALE JEANNETTE: Take the 5 tablespoons reserved Béchamel, mix in 1 egg yolk, 1 cup cream and some sliced cooked mushrooms (optional). Taste for seasoning and heat thoroughly.

7 egg yolks
Salt
Pepper
Nutmeg
Onion, grated
1 calf's brain*

7 egg whites, stiffly beaten
½ cup peas, cooked
Butter
Bread crumbs
1 egg yolk
1 cup cream

*In place of calf's brain substitute cooked, diced sweetbreads. Or use a short ½ cup grated Parmesan cheese in place of either.

SUGGESTED WINES:
White Burgundy — Clos de Vougeot
Red Rhône — Tavel

TOAST BRISTOL

Poach a very fresh calf's brain in salted water, skin and cut in slices about ½ inch thick. Fry slices of white bread in butter, then spread thinly with Colman's mustard, top with the slices of the calf's brain and anchovy filets. Sprinkle with a few drops of oil taken from the anchovy tin and some bread crumbs. Set under broiler to burn lightly. Serve hot.

SUGGESTED WINES:
White Bordeaux — Graves
White Burgundy — Meursault

TOAST NAPOLITAINE

Fry slices of white bread in butter, cover each piece of toast with sliced tomatoes, place anchovy filets on top, sprinkle with grated cheese and a few drops of oil or butter. Broil until heated through. Serve hot.

SUGGESTED WINES:
White Loire — Pouilly-Fumé
Red Rhône — Châteauneuf-du-Pape

TOAST VILLEROY

Cut cooked white chicken meat in small strips, slice cooked mushrooms, julienne some cooked ham and mix into White Wine Sauce (page 27). Spoon over slices of white bread fried in butter and garnish with asparagus tips.

SUGGESTED WINES:
White Rhine (Hock) – Riesling
White Burgundy – Pouilly-Fuissé

VOL-AU-VENT TOULOUSIENNE

To a Sauce Américaine (page 18) add cooked, diced chicken, cooked shrimp and lobster meat, also lightly poached oysters and small pieces of poached fish. To make sauce spicier, add a little dry white wine, as well as Basic Brown Sauce (page 10). Heat and serve in small vol-au-vent cases.

SUGGESTED WINES:
White Burgundy – Macon
White Orvieto – Secco

WELSH RAREBIT

Put a thick slice of Cheddar cheese in a heavy saucepan. Add ½ cup beer, some ground pepper, both black and red, and cook over a low

heat, stirring constantly until cheese melts. Serve over toast.
If served with a poached egg on top, it is called Golden Buck. With slices of fried bacon over the cheese mixture it is a Yorkshire Rarebit.

SUGGESTED WINES:
White Bordeaux – Graves
White Swiss – Neuchâtel
Red Rhône – Tavel

fish

The gourmet possibilities of fish are often neglected. However, not only does fish offer a nutritious and highly delectable way to bring variety into the daily menus of the household; it is also a welcome change for more formal occasions. The recipes included here are equally appropriate as one of the preliminary courses or as the main course of a dinner party.

CRÊPES WITH SEAFOOD FAVORITE

Make large thin Crêpes (page 11) about 1½ times the normal size. Prepare a Sauce Américaine (page 18) and stir in cream. Take some cooked, diced lobster and/or crabmeat and/or shrimp and mix into sauce américaine. Put several tablespoons of the mixture on each crêpe, fold crêpe over the filling and place in an oven-proof, buttered serving dish. Cover all the crêpes with remaining Sauce Américaine. Sprinkle with finely chopped parsley and a smidgeon of grated Parmesan. Place under preheated broiler to take on color.

SUGGESTED WINES:
White Bordeaux – Graves
White Burgundy – Montrachet
Red Rhône – Tavel

FILET OF FISH FLORENTINE

Poach the filets of fish, dry, and keep warm. Cook some young spinach leaves, press well, so that they no longer contain any liquid. Butter ovenproof serving dish and arrange spinach leaves to a depth of about one inch on the bottom. Cover with fish filets, then the entire dish with Sauce Mornay (page 25). Sprinkle lavishly with grated cheese and a little melted butter. Set under broiler to gratiner.

SUGGESTED WINES:
White Rhine (Hock) – Riesling
White Rhine (Hock) – Liebfraumilch
White Bordeaux – Graves
White Burgundy – Chablis

GRATINÉ OF LOBSTER

Take medium-size cooked lobsters, remove meat, cut into slices, and sauté lightly in butter with some sliced mushrooms and chopped onion. Place in a flame-proof serving dish and keep warm.

Melt 1 tablespoon Lobster Butter (page 14) in a saucepan and mix with 3 tablespoons Velouté (page 28) made with fish stock. Stir while while it heats through. Add 1 tablespoon warmed cognac and ignite. Mix in salt, pepper, and a dash of Colman's mustard, some cream mixed with an egg yolk and combine well. Pour sauce over lobster, sprinkle lavishly with grated Gruyère cheese and a few drops of melted butter. Place under a preheated broiler until well colored.

Shrimp, crabmeat, crayfish, scampi, or other seafood may be used instead of lobster.

SUGGESTED WINES:
White Bordeaux — Graves
White Rhône — Hermitage
White Burgundy — Meursault
White Burgundy — Pouilly-Fuissé

LOBSTER THERMIDOR

Split 1 cooked lobster down the middle. Remove the meat and cut into medium-size dice. Then wash and dry shells. Make a thin Velouté (page 28) with fish stock, stir in cream mixed with egg yolk and a good pinch of Colman's mustard. Season with salt and pepper and spoon a little sauce in bottom of shells, cover with sliced mushrooms, lightly sautéed, and the diced lobster. Add more sauce, enough to cover lobster mixture. Sprinkle with grated Gruyère cheese and a few drops of melted butter. Place under a preheated broiler to gratiner.

SUGGESTED WINES:
White Bordeaux — Graves
White Rhône — Hermitage
White Burgundy — Meursault

LOBSTER AU WHISKEY

For 2 portions take the meat from 1 medium-size lobster, slice the meat and sauté in butter. Add for each lobster 1 tablespoon bourbon whiskey and ignite. Keep warm. At the same time make the following sauce: 4 heaping tablespoons fish velouté, pepper, salt, a little more bourbon and 1 egg yolk mixed into ½ cup cream. Place the lobster meat in a buttered serving dish, cover with the sauce, sprinkle with melted butter, and set under hot broiler to glaze.

SUGGESTED WINES:
White Moselle — Piesporter
White Alsatian — Gewürztraminer
White Burgundy — Meursault

MERIDON OF SCAMPI IN DILL

Combine cooked scampi or crayfish or shrimp with dill sauce made of Fish Stock (page 28). Press hot cooked rice into a buttered ring mold, turn out on a serving dish, and place the sauced seafood in the center.

SUGGESTED WINES:
White Loire — Sancerre
White Burgundy — Montrachet

MUSSELS À LA PAULETTE

Follow recipe for Oysters à la Paulette (page 95), replacing oysters with mussels.

SUGGESTED WINES:
White Loire — Muscadet
White Loire — Sancerre
White Loire — Vouvray
White Burgundy — Pouilly-Fuissé

fish

MUSSELS MARINIÈRE

Clean a large quantity of very fresh mussels in shells. Cook in boiling Fish Stock (page 28) along with lemon juice, a lot of finely chopped onion, freshly ground pepper and some dry white wine. When shells open, the mussels are done. Serve in soup plates.

SUGGESTED WINES:
White Loire – Muscadet
White Loire – Sancerre
White Loire – Vouvray
White Burgundy – Pouilly-Fuissé

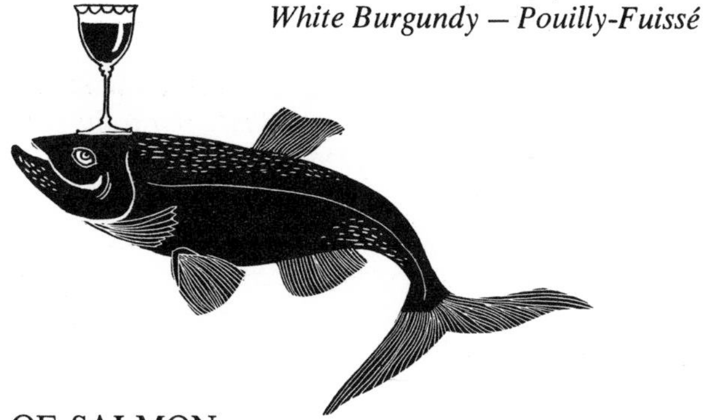

KEDGEREE OF SALMON

Heat pieces of poached salmon in butter, bind with Curry Sauce (page 22), mix with white rice and decorate with quarters of warm hard-boiled eggs. Other poached fish can be used equally as well.

SUGGESTED WINES:
White Alsatian – Traminer
White Rhône – Hermitage
Red Rhône – Châteauneuf-du-Pape
Red Rhône – Tavel

POACHED SALMON DIEPPOISE

Poach a whole or ½, well-cleaned salmon in this court bouillon. Combine enough water to cover fish, ½ lemon, chopped leeks, chopped onions, chopped carrots, parsley. Boil until liquid is somewhat reduced. Add salmon and poach until cooked through. Remove fish from liquid and skin immediately. Also scrape off any grayish surface completely.
Place napkin on serving platter and salmon on top. Serve with Sauce Béarnaise (page 19) to which well drained capers, small cooked shrimp, and poached oysters have been added.

SUGGESTED WINES:
White Bordeaux – Graves
White Burgundy – Clos des Mouches
White Burgundy – Pouilly-Fuissé

SCALLOPS MORNAY

Cut sea scallops in slices, or bay scallops whole, and poach in dry white wine until cooked through. Drain and place in coquille shells along with a few sliced, cooked mushrooms. Cover with Sauce Mornay (page 25) and place under a preheated broiler to take on color. Sauce Mornay can be replaced by Curry Sauce (page 22).

SUGGESTED WINES:
White Bordeaux – Graves
White Rhône – Hermitage
White Burgundy – Pouilly-Fuissé

SCAMPI À LA BROCHE

For this recipe you can also use shrimp or other seafood. Pierce on a skewer the raw or poached seafood, rub it slightly with garlic, turn in flour, then in melted butter (optional in chopped parsley) and place under hot broiler. Serve with Sauce Américaine (page 18) on the side.

SUGGESTED WINES:
White Burgundy – Meursault
White Burgundy – Musigny
White Burgundy – Pouilly-Fuissé
White Burgundy – Puligny-Montrachet

SHRIMP BORDELAISE

Cook shrimp with salt in milk and ½ water, seasoned with lemon juice. Drain, peel and devein. Sauté shrimp in a little butter and keep warm while you make the following sauce: For 1 pound peeled shrimp; melt 2 tablespoons butter in a saucepan. Stir in 1½ tablespoons flour smoothly and cook until slightly brown. Add grated onion, salt, pepper, paprika, 1½ cup Basic Brown Sauce (page 10), 1 cup dry red wine, 1 chopped bay leaf, parsley, tarragon and thyme. Simmer for 30 minutes. Add consommé if too thick; if too thin, bring to a boil and add a little Beurre Manié (page 10). Strain, then add the shrimp, some freshly chopped parsley and cooked mushrooms, sliced. Heat through before serving.

SUGGESTED WINES:
White Bordeaux – Graves
White Burgundy – Corton-Charlemagne
Red Bordeaux (Claret) – Pomerol

CURRIED SHRIMP INDIENNE

Cook shrimp, peel and clean and sauté lightly in butter. Make a Curry Sauce (page 22) (see to it that the sauce is not too thick), add the shrimp, and simmer for about 10 minutes. Then add some cream to the curry sauce, a few raisins, chopped almonds, and serve with hot rice.

SUGGESTED WINES:
White Bordeaux – Margaux
White Burgundy – Nuits Saint Georges

FILET OF SOLE ANTOINETTE

Poach in advance 6 medium-sized filets of sole in white wine. Drain, pat dry, and keep warm. Heat butter in pan until it sizzles, add tomatoes, celery, onion, mushrooms, tarragon. Stir well, add white wine and brandy, salt, and pepper. Stir in sour cream and let simmer some 5 minutes. Pour this sauce over poached filets of sole, heat through and serve with rice. Serves 3.

6 filets of sole of medium size
2 tablespoons of butter
1 tablespoon of chopped onions
Tarragon
Salt
Pepper
½ cup sliced mushrooms
2 cups peeled, coarsely chopped tomatoes
Consommé
1 cup sour cream
½ glass white wine
Few drops brandy

SUGGESTED WINES:
White Rhine (Hock) – Johannisberg
White Rhine (Hock) – Liebfraumilch
White Moselle – Bernkastel

fish

FILET OF SOLE CAFÉ DE PARIS

Poach filets of sole in dry white wine until cooked through. Drain and reserve the liquid. Keep the filets warm in a serving dish.
Make a Velouté (page 28), with some of the reserved liquid and Fish Stock (page 28), season with salt and pepper, and stir in cream mixed with egg yolk or Sabayon (page 18). Also add some sliced mushrooms, mussels and/or raw oysters. Simmer sauce for a moment, pour over filets, sprinkle surface with a few drops of melted butter, place under preheated broiler until well glazed.

SUGGESTED WINES:
White Bordeaux — Graves
White Burgundy — Chablis
White Burgundy — Clos de Vougeot

FILET OF SOLE CHAMBORD

For 4 persons take 4 medium-size filets of sole and poach in ½ consommé, ½ port wine. Make the following sauce: 8 tablespoons Sauce Américaine (page 18) mixed well into 4 tablespoons Sauce Béarnaise (page 19), adding ½ tablespoon cognac. Place the well-dried filets in serving dish, top with diced, cooked lobster meat, and cover with the sauce. Serve rice on the side.

SUGGESTED WINES:
White Bordeaux — Margaux
White Burgundy — Batard Montrachet
White Burgundy — Clos de Vougeot

FILET OF SOLE DEAUVILLE

Poach filets of sole in dry white wine to which a few drops of cognac have been added. Drain. Arrange in a buttered serving dish and cover with sliced, cooked mushrooms. Pour sauce Béarnaise (page 19) over fish before serving.

SUGGESTED WINES:
White Alsatian – Gewürztraminer
White Burgundy – Meursault

FILET OF SOLE AU FOIE GRAS

For 4 persons take 8 filets of sole, poach in dry white wine, then dry well with a cloth. Place preheated purée of *foie gras* (tinned) or *foie gras* sliced about ½ inch thick on 4 of the filets, and top with the other 4 filets.

Make a Velouté (page 28) with fish stock and dry white wine, season well with pepper. Add 1 cup cream mixed with 2 egg yolks, or Sabayon (page 18), and cream some cooked sliced mushrooms. Cover the filets with this sauce, which should not be too thick, and sprinkle with a few drops of butter. Set under the hot broiler to glaze until well-browned.

NOTE: Purée of *foie gras* is obtainable in many delicatessen stores in tins of 7 ounces or larger.

SUGGESTED WINES:
White Bordeaux – Barsac
White Bordeaux – Graves
White Burgundy – Montrachet
Red Rhône – Tavel

FILET OF SOLE GINA

Poach filets of sole in dry white wine until cooked through. Drain thoroughly and arrange fish in a buttered serving dish. Top with alternate slices of cooked lobster and sliced ripe tomatoes. Sprinkle with a little bourbon, then cover with Sauce Américaine (page 18) to which a few drops of bourbon have been added. Glaze under a preheated broiler to take on color.

SUGGESTED WINES:
White Rhône – Hermitage
White Burgundy – Corton Charlemagne
White Burgundy – Meursault

FILET OF SOLE HÔTELIÈRE

For 6 persons take 6 thick filets of sole and slice each filet in strips about 1 inch wide. Salt and pepper, turn in finely grated Parmesan cheese and flour. Dip in beaten egg, turn in fine bread crumbs, sauté in butter until golden brown. In a separate pan place meat of 4 large tomatoes, ½ cup chopped onions, 1 fine sliver garlic, lemon juice, chopped parsley, and tarragon, ½ cup Basic Brown Sauce (page 10), ½ cup dry red wine, and simmer for 20 minutes. Pour this sauce into the bottom of the serving dish and arrange the filets on top.

SUGGESTED WINES:
White Rhône – Hermitage
White Beaujolais
Red Rhône – Tavel

FILET OF SOLE LYONNAISE

For 4 persons take 8 small filets of sole, wash, trim on sides, and flatten a little bit, dry well, then salt and pepper. Make a Forcemeat of Chicken (page 13, ⅔ of quantities in recipe will be sufficient). With a spatula spread the forcemeat on each filet, place in buttered pan, add consommé to immerse as much of the filets as possible without wetting the forcemeat. Cover the pan with thick paper dipped in oil. Place in oven and simmer for 30 minutes at about 350° F, adding a little consommé now and then to replace the liquid which has evaporated. Serve with Sauce Américaine (page 18) or Sauce Béarnaise (page 19) on the side.

SUGGESTED WINES:
White Bordeaux — Margaux
White Burgundy — Macon
Red Rhône — Tavel

FILET OF SOLE MEXICAINE

For 6 people take 6 good-size filets of sole. Turn in flour, seasoned with salt and pepper. Sauté in butter. In a separate pan, fry in oil 6 small peeled bananas sprinkled with curry powder. Take 2 small tins of corn niblets, drain well, bind with cream and heat. Cover the bottom of the serving dish with the creamed corn niblets, then top with the filets of sole, and garnish all around with the bananas.

SUGGESTED WINES:
White Alsatian — Traminer
White Bordeaux — Graves
White Burgundy — Meursault

fish

FILET OF SOLE ROYAL

For each person take 2 small filets of sole. Salt and pepper and roll each one around a thick slice of cooked lobster (which should be the same width as the filets). Bind each filet with a thread and poach in Fish Stock (page 28). When cooked, drain, remove thread, pad dry, and place on a serving dish. Cover with Sauce Américaine (page 18), decorate with slices of truffle, and serve with a garland of rice.

SUGGESTED WINES:
White Rhône – Hermitage
White Burgundy – Meursault
White Burgundy – Puligny-Montrachet

FILET OF SOLE À LA RUSSE

For 4 persons take 8 small filets of sole, wash, flatten a little bit, salt and pepper. Melt some butter in pan, add the filets and enough consommé to cover. Top the pan with a lid, until cooked. Remove the filets and dry with a cloth. Place on warm serving platter, cover with Dill Sauce (page 22), decorate with cooked shrimp and a garland of rice.

SUGGESTED WINES:
White Alsatian – Traminer
White Bordeaux – Graves
White Burgundy – Pouilly-Fuissé

FILET OF SOLE VÉRONIQUE

For 4 persons turn 4 large filets of sole in flour and sauté in melted butter mixed with a little grated onion and lemon juice until fish takes on a little color. Add some dry white wine and continue to cook until filets are done. Remove filets from pan to a serving dish and keep warm. Mix 4 tablespoons Velouté (page 28) made with fish stock into liquid remaining in pan. Remove from heat and stir in whipped cream. Pour sauce over filets and garnish with plenty of sautéed seedless grapes. Place under a preheated broiler a moment to glaze.

SUGGESTED WINES:
White Loire – Muscadet
White Burgundy – Chablis
White Burgundy – Pouilly-Fuissé

fish

SOLE MEUNIÈRE

Turn sole or filets of sole in flour and sauté in butter until cooked through. Place on a hot serving platter and keep warm. Add a good deal more butter to pan, stir in some salt, pepper, chopped parsley, and lemon juice. The moment the butter starts to turn black and gives off a nut-like fragrance, pour over the cooked sole. Sprinkle with more lemon juice and chopped parsley and serve immediately. Sauce Béarnaise (page 19) can be served on the side.

SUGGESTED WINES:
White Burgundy – Batard Montrachet
White Burgundy – Clos des Mouches
White Burgundy – Pouilly-Fuissé

SOLE À LA RUE

For 4 persons take 8 medium-size filets. Salt and pepper and poach in dry white wine. Take 1½ pounds fresh mushrooms and cook in ½ consommé, ½ water, adding ½ a lemon. Liquid should just cover mushrooms. When tender, blend in the electric blender. Mix the purée with a Velouté (page 28) made with mushroom stock, adding a few drops dry white wine. Place the mushroom purée on bottom of a buttered, oven-proof baking dish and cover with the filets of sole. Pour a thin Sauce Mornay (page 25) over the filets. Sprinkle with grated cheese and a few drops of butter. Place under preheated broiler to take on color.

SUGGESTED WINES:
White Loire – Pouilly-Fumé
White Bordeaux – Barsac
White Bordeaux – Graves

TROUT TYROLIENNE

Clean trout well and dip into milk, then turn in flour, minced with salt and pepper. Place ample butter in pan and when hot, sauté the trout. When cooked, remove from pan, place on serving dish, sprinkle with lemon juice, and keep warm. To the remaining liquid in the pan add some blanched, split almonds, more fresh butter, and more lemon juice. Brown the butter and when foaming, pour over trout and serve at once.

SUGGESTED WINES:
White Rhine (Hock) – Johannisberg
White Rhine (Hock) – Liebfraumilch
White Alsatian – Traminer
White Loire – Muscadet
White Loire – Sancerre
White Loire – Vouvray
White Burgundy – Pouilly-Fuissé

fowl

Years ago, chicken poultry was expensive, its appearance on the menu was saved for special occasions. Now most poultry has become extremely inexpensive in comparison with many other meats. That does not, however, alter the fact that, prepared in an interesting and imaginative fashion, fowl is ideal as the main course for the most festive party. It is somewhat lighter than a meat course and entirely appropriate for either luncheon or dinner.
When fresh poultry is available, it should be selected for roasting or frying; frozen poultry is better for stews. The tip of the breast bone of a young tender fowl should be pliable, the breast should be full and well-developed. Approximately one-fourth of the weight of a chicken represents usable meat.

CHICKEN À LA BASQUE

For 2 portions take a medium-size chicken and cut in 4 pieces. Salt and pepper, turn in flour. Squeeze out juice and seeds of tomatoes and dice. Take a heavy pan and rub the bottom with garlic, add butter. When the butter is sizzling add chicken and brown on all sides. Add tomatoes, green and red peppers sliced julienne, sliced raw mushrooms, sliced eggplant, diced ham. Stir well, then add dry white wine and chopped parsley. Place lid on pan and cook slowly for about 30 minutes. Rectify seasoning, place chicken on serving dish and cover with the vegetable mixture. Serve with rice on the side.

1 medium-size chicken	3 green peppers
Salt	3 red peppers
Pepper	¼ pound mushrooms
Flour	1 medium eggplant
4 tomatoes	½ cup diced ham
Garlic	1½ cups dry white wine
Butter	Parsley, chopped

SUGGESTED WINES:
White Bordeaux — Graves
White Burgundy — Pouilly-Fuissé
Red Bordeaux (Claret) — Saint Emilion
Red Bordeaux (Claret) — Saint Julien

BLANQUETTE OF CHICKEN

Cut a broiler into 4 parts, season with salt and pepper, sauté in butter to a light brown color, then proceed as for Blanquette of Veal (page 176).

SUGGESTED WINES:
White Loire — Pouilly-Fumé
White Burgundy — Montrachet
Red Bordeaux (Claret) — Château-Margaux
Red Rhône — Châteauneuf-du-Pape

fowl

CHICKEN BREASTS FINANCIÈRE

Salt and pepper breasts of chicken, sauté in butter until tender, then skin. Return to pan. Add Basic Brown Sauce (page 10) blended with a little consommé (enough to cover), dry white wine to taste, chopped parsley and tarragon, julienne of cooked ham, sliced cooked mushrooms, and pitted olives. Serve piping hot with boiled or gratin potatoes.

SUGGESTED WINES:
White Burgundy – Montrachet
Red Bordeaux (Claret) – Château-Margaux
Red Burgundy – Clos de Vougeot

CHICKEN CASSEROLE PARISIENNE

Cut a broiling chicken in quarters, salt and pepper, and sauté in butter until well browned. In a heavy pan, fry some little cubes of bacon until almost crisp. Add 1 tablespoon oil, 2 large onions, sliced, 10 raw potato balls, some diced carrot and celery root, a few mushrooms, small white onions, chopped parsley and tarragon and cook for about 5 minutes. Add cooked green peas and the sautéed chicken. Pour in a mixture of Basic Brown Sauce (page 10), and white wine, half and half (1 cup). Add enough consommé to cover ingredients. Cover and place in moderate (300° F) oven until vegetables are tender.

SUGGESTED WINES:
White Loire – Pouilly-Fumé
White Bordeaux – Graves
White Burgundy – Clos de Vougeot
Red Bordeaux (Claret) – Château-Margaux

CHICKEN À LA CRÈME BARONESSE

Cut a large chicken in 4, salt and pepper, sauté until light brown, then add 1 cup dry white wine. Cover and simmer slowly. When nearly tender add sliced fresh mushrooms and some grated onions. Make a Velouté (page 28) with consommé or mushroom stock (about 1½ cups of Velouté are required). Add an equal amount of cream and cook a few minutes. Place the chicken in a serving dish, pour sauce over it and garnish with slices of truffles or tarragon leaves. Serve with rice or noodles.

SUGGESTED WINES:
White Bordeaux — Graves
White Beaujolais — Moulin-à-Vent
White Burgundy — Montrachet

CHICKEN CRÉOLE

Cut a broiling chicken in quarters, salt and pepper, dust with flour, and sauté in half butter and half oil until tender. Remove from pan, take out as many bones as possible. To the pan add 4 to 5 skinned and crushed fresh tomatoes, some finely chopped chili to taste, about 5 tablespoons chopped onion, a generous amount of chopped parsley and geen peas also a sliver of garlic. Simmer until well blended. Serve over chicken.

SUGGESTED WINES:
White Burgundy — Musigny
White Burgundy — Pouilly-Fuissé
Red Bordeaux (Claret) — Château-Margaux

fowl

CURRIED CHICKEN INDIENNE

Cut up a broiler in 4 pieces, salt and pepper, sauté in butter until half cooked, (chicken may be poached in consommé instead of sautéed). Pull off skin and simmer chicken for about 30 minutes in Curry Sauce (page 22). During the last few minutes, toss in some cooked small onions, peanuts or almonds, diced pineapple, and raisins. Serve with rice and chutney on the side.

SUGGESTED WINES:
White Burgundy — Meursault
Red Bordeaux (Claret) — Pomerol
Red Burgundy — Beaune

CHICKEN À LA DIANE

Cut a broiling chicken in quarters, salt and pepper and sauté in butter with chopped onion, parsley, and tarragon leaves. Purée some cooked mushrooms in electric blender, stir in a little dry white wine, Basic Brown Sauce (page 10) and bind with some Velouté (page 28) made with mushroom stock, adding cream. Remove chicken to serving dish and pour the heated sauce over chicken. Shower with chopped parsley before serving.

SUGGESTED WINES:
White Bordeaux — Graves
White Beaujolais — Moulin-à-Vent
White Burgundy — Montrachet

CHICKEN FARCIE AMBASSADEUR

Make up ½ the quantity of Chicken or Veal Forcemeat (page 13) for 1 large chicken. With your finger loosen the skin over the breast and thighs, push as much of the forcemeat between the skin and flesh as you possibly can. At the same time, work in thin slices of truffle. Sprinkle the cavity of the chicken with salt and insert 1 whole large onion. Tie up the chicken in a napkin or cheesecloth, place in boiling consommé, then simmer until tender. Lift chicken out of broth, remove cloth, and keep warm.

Prepare the following sauce: Make a Velouté (page 28) with chicken consommé, stir in liquid from the can of truffles, salt, pepper, and sherry to taste. Add 1 cup cream mixed with 2 egg yolks and strain. Carve the chicken with care and arrange on serving dish. Pour sauce over the entire chicken and garnish all around with little heaps of cooked, fresh peas, green beans, and rice in little heaps, grilled tomatoes, and asparagus tips. Garnish each piece of chicken with a thin slice of truffle. This will serve 4 to 6 people.

SUGGESTED WINES:
White Burgundy – Montrachet
White Burgundy – Pouilly-Fuissé
Red Bordeaux (Claret) – Pomerol

fowl

CHICKEN MIRAMAR

Cut a broiling chicken in quarters and marinate for 2 to 3 hours in a mixture of oil, vinegar, salt, pepper, thyme, tarragon, bay leaf, sliced carrots, and onion. Remove from marinade and pat dry. Melt some butter in a heavy pan, add chicken and brown on all sides. Pour in a little consommé and the marinade in which chicken steeped. Simmer until tender. Dry, remove to serving dish, and keep warm. Make a Velouté (page 28) with consommé (about 6 tablespoons), add ½ cup Basic Brown Sauce (page 10), grated onion and a few drops of vinegar and some prepared French mustard. Add cream mixed with egg yolk to taste, slices of lightly sautéed mushrooms, salt and pepper. Reheat and pour over chicken. Serve with rice mixed with crushed peanuts.

SUGGESTED WINES:
White Burgundy — Meursault
Red Bordeaux (Claret) — Château-Margaux
Red Burgundy — Pommard

PAPRIKA CHICKEN

For 2 portions cut a broiler in 4, salt and pepper, turn in flour. Place ¼ cup butter and ¼ cup oil in a heavy pan, add 3 thick slices bacon, diced. When hot add 4 large, sliced onions, and the chicken. Brown well on all sides, mix in a generous amount of paprika, add 5 ripe tomatoes skinned and sliced, 1 tablespoon tomato purée, and enough consommé just to cover. Place the lid on the pan, bring to boil, then simmer 45 minutes or until chicken is tender.
Make a small amount of Velouté (page 28) with consommé to

which add ample paprika and part of the liquid in which the chicken was cooked (dry white wine is optional). Place chicken, along with bacon and vegetables, in the sauce. Stir in cream, chopped parsley (tarragon optional) to taste. Heat well. This dish should be accompanied by spaghetti, noodles, or Spaetzle (page 100).

SUGGESTED WINES:
White Burgundy — Batard Montrachet
Red Bordeaux (Claret) — Pomerol
Red Burgundy — Pommard

CHICKEN IN RED WINE

For 2 persons cut a broiling chicken in quarters, salt and pepper, dust with flour. Sauté in half butter, and half oil until well browned. Put a handful of diced bacon in a heavy pan along with a pinch of thyme and crushed bay leaf, some chopped parsley, 1 cup fresh medium-size mushrooms, a handful of small white onions, and a little crushed garlic. Cook until lightly brown. Add chicken, 3 to 4 skinned and sliced tomatoes, and cover with a mixture of half dry red wine, ¼ consommé and ¼ Basic Brown Sauce (page 10). Simmer about 30 minutes, then add some small potato balls. Cover. When potatoes are done, the dish is ready to serve. If the sauce seems too thin, thicken with a little Beurre Manié (page 10).

SUGGESTED WINES:
White Rhône — Hermitage
Red Bordeaux (Claret) — Château-Margaux
Red Rhône — Châteauneuf-du-Pape
Red Beaujolais

fowl

CHICKEN RIGOLETTO

For 6 portions take 2 to 3 chickens, depending upon size. Clean well and place in boiling consommé. Simmer until tender. Take out of liquid. Cool, skin, cut each chicken into 4 pieces and remove as many bones as possible. Make a Velouté (page 28) with chicken consommé using 5 tablespoons butter and 2½ flour, salt, pepper, juice of 1 lemon. Add 4 egg yolks and 1 cup cream to the Velouté while it is still hot, also 2 to 3 tablespoons Aspic (page 8). Strain. Dip each piece of chicken into the Velouté, then place on a baking sheet which has been lavishly sprinkled with bread crumbs. Place in refrigerator. When set, turn each piece in beaten egg then in bread crumbs, and fry in deep fat until golden brown. Serve with French peas and rice.

SUGGESTED WINES:
White Loire — Vouvray
White Burgundy — Batard Montrachet
Red Bordeaux (Claret) — Saint Emilion

COQ AU RIESLING

Cut a broiling chicken in quarters and sauté in butter until tender. Pull off chicken skin and take out as many bones as possible. Make a Velouté (page 28) with mushroom stock. Add some Riesling or another dry white wine, cream mixed with 1 egg yolk, sliced and lightly sautéed mushrooms. Arrange chicken on a bed of rice and cover with the sauce.

SUGGESTED WINES:
White Rhine (Hock) — Riesling
White Moselle — Piesporter
White Burgundy — Chablis

SUPRÊME OF CHICKEN AUX AMANDES

Cut raw chicken breasts in slices, salt and pepper, remove skin and sauté in butter until tender. Toss in some blanched split almonds. Mix together Velouté (page 28) made with chicken stock, a little dry white wine, and cream. Arrange chicken and almonds on a serving dish and cover with the heated sauce.

SUGGESTED WINES:
White Bordeaux – Grave
White Burgundy – Meursault
Red Rhône – Tavel

SUPRÊME OF CHICKEN BEATRICE

Debone chicken breasts, salt and pepper and sauté in butter along with a little chopped onion until chicken is tender. While the chicken cooks make the following sauce: Mix together and heat 1 cup Basic Brown Sauce (page 10), 1 tablespoon red currant jelly, 2 tablespoons blanched, slivered almonds, a little lemon juice, salt and pepper. Place skinned chicken in sauce and simmer about 10 minutes. Serve with Dauphine Potatoes (page 71) and stringbeans.

SUGGESTED WINES:
White Bordeaux – Graves
White Burgundy – Montrachet
White Burgundy – Pouilly-Fuissé
Red Bordeaux (Claret) – Médoc

fowl

SUPRÊME OF CHICKEN CARMEN

For 4 persons sauté in half oil and half butter 4 breasts of chicken. When cooked, skin, debone, and keep warm. Sauté ¼ pound shrimp in the same pan, with 1 or 2 green peppers, cut in julienne, ample amount of onion rings. When vegetables are tender, skim off all excess fat and place mixture on top of the chicken breasts. Make a Sauce Américaine (page 18) adding some cream and pour over the breasts. Sprinkle with cheese and brown under the broiler.

SUGGESTED WINES:
White Clairette du Languedoc
White Rhône — Hermitage
White Burgundy — Meursault
Red Rhône — Châteauneuf-du-Pape

SUPRÊME OF CHICKEN DEAUVILLE

For 4 persons take 4 medium-size breasts of chicken. Sált and pepper and sauté in butter until lightly browned. Add half consommé and half dry white wine to cover, put a lid on, and simmer until tender. Remove from pan, skin, debone, and set aside to keep warm. Make the following sauce: To a Velouté (page 28) made with half consommé and half liquor from the oysters, add 2 tablespoons dry white wine, lemon juice, salt, pepper, 1 tablespoon grated onion, 4 to 5 tablespoons sour cream, and mix well. Then add the oysters and simmer until the edges start to curl. Pour over the chicken.

cont'd

4 medium-size breasts of chicken	Dry white wine
Salt	Velouté
Pepper	24 oysters in their liquor
Butter	Lemon juice
Consommé	Onion
	Sour cream

SUGGESTED WINES:
White Alsatian – Traminer
White Burgundy – Macon
White Burgundy – Meursault
Red Bordeaux (Claret) – Château Margaux

SUPRÊME OF CHICKEN MARIE-LOUISE

Salt and pepper chicken breasts and sauté in butter until cooked through. Remove skin and bones, cover with Sauce Béarnaise (page 19), combined with small cooked shrimp or lobster meat and lightly sautéed mushroom slices. Garnish serving dish with asparagus tips. Serve with rice.

SUGGESTED WINES:
White Burgundy – Corton Charlemagne
Red Rhône – Tavel
Red Burgundy – Chambolle-Musigny
Red Burgundy – Volnay

SUPRÊME OF CHICKEN MEDICI

Sauté breasts of chicken in butter, flavored with a little garlic, salt and pepper, until nicely brown. Add some chopped onion and a little dry white wine. Simmer for 20 minutes or until chicken is tender. Debone and skin. While chicken cooks, heat some butter in a saucepan, stir in some slices of gruyère cheese, and cook until it melts. Add some dry white wine, cream, and a little consommé. Fry slices of white bread in butter (1 slice for each breast of chicken), cover the fried toast with a thin slice of lightly sautéed ham, top ham with chicken breast, and pour over enough sauce to cover the chicken. Serve with grilled tomatoes or purée of spinach.

SUGGESTED WINES:
White Bordeaux – Margaux
White Burgundy – Montrachet
Red Bordeaux (Claret) – Château Margaux
Red Rhône – Tavel

SUPRÊME OF CHICKEN À LA SUISSE

Sauté chicken breasts in butter until cooked through. Remove bones and skin and place chicken in a buttered flame-proof serving dish. Cover with Sauce Mornay (page 25). Sprinkle with grated cheese. Place under a preheated broiler to gratiner. Serve with noodles or rice.
Variation: Arrange chicken breasts on a layer of cooked spinach leaves. Cover with sauce Mornay and gratiner.

SUGGESTED WINES:
White Bordeaux – Graves
White Burgundy – Montrachet
White Burgundy – Pouilly-Fuissé
Red Bordeaux (Claret) – Médoc

SUPRÊME OF CHICKEN VÉRONIQUE

Cut raw chicken breasts in slices, remove skin, then salt and pepper and sauté in butter. Sauté a few slices of ham and place in bottom of serving dish. Cover with chicken slices and top with cooked seedless grapes. Sprinkle with cognac and ignite. Pour over Basic Brown Sauce (page 10) into which a little butter has been beaten. Taste for seasoning. Serve hot.

SUGGESTED WINES:
White Alsatian — Gewürztraminer
White Bordeaux — Graves
White Burgundy — Batard Montrachet
Red Bordeaux (Claret) — Pomerol

DUCK WITH CHERRIES

Follow recipe for Duck à L'orange (page 140), substituting red cherries for oranges and cherry brandy in place of orange liqueur.

SUGGESTED WINES:
White Alsatian — Traminer
Red Bordeaux (Claret) — Pomerol
Red Burgundy — Beaune
Red Burgundy — Clos de Vougeot

DUCK LIVERS BASQUE STYLE

For 2 persons take 8 duck livers. Skin, clean, and slice. Turn in flour and sauté lightly in hot butter with grated onion until cooked. Remove livers from pan and keep warm. To the same pan with all remaining liquids, add 2 large mushrooms, sliced, 1 tablespoon raisins, ½ tablespoon cognac and ignite. Then add 2 tablespoons Basic Brown Sauce (page 10), salt, pepper, 2 tablespoons cream. Stir well and mix with the duck livers. Serve hot with large fried croutons.

SUGGESTED WINES:
Red Bordeaux (Claret) – Saint Emilion
Red Burgundy – Chambolle-Musigny
Red Burgundy – Vosne-Romanée

DUCK MELANIE

Melt a little butter in a large, heavy, flame-proof pan. Salt and pepper the duck and brown on all sides. Toss in some chopped onions and carrots. Pour in a little consommé, cover and roast in a preheated 325°F oven for 45 to 60 minutes. Place duck on serving platter and keep warm. Strain off pan juices, return to pan and add 3 apples, cored, pared, and sliced, a handful of raisins and some fresh seedless grapes. Cook on top of stove until apples are tender. Mix together the fruits, add some sour cream, salt and pepper to taste. Serve over the carved duck.

SUGGESTED WINES:
White Alsatian – Traminer
Red Bordeaux (Claret) – Pomerol
Red Burgundy – Beaune
Red Burgundy – Clos de Vougeot

DUCK À L'ORANGE

Clean a duck and stuff 1 or 2 whole oranges (prick skins with a fork) into cavity. Season with salt and pepper. Brown the duck in butter on all sides, adding carrots, onions, tomatoes, then roast in preheated hot (350° F) oven until done. Make the following sauce: Combine 1 cup Basic Brown Sauce (page 10) with juice 1 orange, about 2 to 3 tablespoons Grand Marnier, salt and pepper to taste, some fine julienne of orange rind. Reduce somewhat, strain, heat again and if necessary, thicken with Beurre Manié (page 10). Sprinkle duck lavishly with half cognac, half Grand Marnier and ignite. To serve, carve, place on a serving dish, pour half the sauce over the duck meat, garnish all around and on top with orange sections. Serve the remainders of the sauce on the side.
A mixed salad is suggested, also shoestring potatoes, French peas, or stringbeans.

SUGGESTED WINES:
White Burgundy – Corton Charlemagne
Red Bordeaux (Claret) – Pomerol
Red Rhône – Hermitage
Red Burgundy – Clos de Vougeot

SALMIS OF DUCK

For about 6 to 8 servings take 2 ducks, clean well, season with salt and pepper inside and out. Brown the ducks on all sides in butter, adding onions, carrots, thyme, and bay leaf. Then roast ducks in a preheated hot (350° F) oven until done. Remove and skin. Carve only the breasts and keep warm. Sauté duck livers or chicken livers

in butter and dry red wine. Put through the meat grinder using the finest blade together with all the remaining meat stripped from the ducks. To this purée add egg yolks, some Basic Brown Sauce (page 10) thickened with Beurre Manié (page 10); (chopped truffles optional). Add a little cognac, port wine, salt and pepper, and simmer for a few minutes. Stir constantly while the mixture is being reheated. Take a 2-day-old loaf of dark bread and shape it like a dome. With a spatula spread the reheated purée on top and all around the loaf. The breast of duck which was reserved should be sliced into lengthwise strips 1-inch wide and arranged around and against the dome. The bread is not to be eaten.

2 ducks
Salt
Pepper
Onions
Carrots
Thyme
Bay leaf
6 or 8 duck livers or
10 to 12 chicken livers
Butter
½ cup dry red wine
3 egg yolks
Basic brown sauce
Beurre manié
Truffles (optional)
Cognac
Port wine
Loaf dark bread
Oranges
Red cherries

SAUCE:

Make a somewhat thickened Madeira Sauce (page 24) and pour over the dome just before serving. Garnish the platter with segments of oranges and red cherries. Lovely *grand pièce* for buffet.

CHAUD-FROID OF DUCK:

Prepare the entire dish as for salmis of duck, but instead of pouring Madeira sauce over the dome, cover it with Aspic (page 8) and let it set in the refrigerator. Serve with Cumberland Sauce (page 21). The chaud-froid of duck is an excellent dish for a cold buffet.

SUGGESTED WINES:
Red Bordeaux (Claret) – Cos D'Estournel
Red Rhône – Côte Rôtie
Red Burgundy – Vosne-Romanée

fowl

ROAST GOOSE

Clean an 8- to 10-pound goose. Sprinkle both inside and out with plenty of salt. Pare 2 or 3 apples and place in the cavity. Pour boiling water in a shallow roasting pan, enough to fill pan about two-thirds full and place the goose in the water, breast side down. Roast in a preheated, 450° to 500°F oven for about 10 minutes, then reduce to 325°F or lower, and roast 3½ to 4 hours or until tender. During roasting, turn goose every 20 minutes from one side to the other. Remove fat that comes to the top of the water. As water evaporates, replace with more boiling water. For the last 30 minutes turn goose breast side up and baste every 5 minutes with the boiling water. This makes the skin very brown and crisp.
Serve with Red Cabbage (page 67), whipped potatoes, Basic Brown Sauce (page 10) and applesauce.

SUGGESTED WINES:
Red Rhône – Côte Rôtie
Red Burgundy – Clos de Vougeot
Red Burgundy – Volnay
Red Sparkling Burgundy

GROUSE

Proceed as for Roast Partridge Alsacienne (page 144).

SUGGESTED WINES:
Red Bordeaux (Claret) – Médoc
Red Burgundy – Gevrey-Chambertin
Red Burgundy – Richebourg
Red Burgundy – Vosne-Romanée

GUINEA HEN SAINT HUBERT

Take a young guinea hen, place in heavy pan with hot butter and brown on all sides. Add consommé to reach to about half the height of the hen and roast in hot oven, basting frequently.
In the meantime fry 1 large crouton in butter and when hen is done, set on crouton and place on serving platter. Sprinkle with cognac and ignite.
Pour Game Sauce (page 22) over the bird, and serve with Dauphine Potatoes (page 71) and French peas or sauerkraut and mashed potatoes.

SUGGESTED WINES:
White Alsatian – Gewürztraminer
Red Rhône – Hermitage
Red Burgundy – Volnay

ROAST PARTRIDGE ALSACIENNE

The important point is to choose young birds. The claws of young birds are yellow in color in contrast to older birds which have grayish claws.
Clean birds well. Set aside livers, hearts, stomachs, and necks (chopped coarsely), adding consommé to cover and simmer until liquid is reduced to half. Salt and pepper partridge inside and out, place ¼ of a raw apple and a medium-size onion in the cavity. Bard the breast completely with lard and bind with a thread. Brown butter in heavy pan, add the birds, a little consommé, dry white wine, bay leaf and onion, and roast in a hot oven, (400°F) starting with one side, then the other, without a lid for about 20 minutes. Then set

birds on their backs and roast another 10 minutes. Serve with Game Sauce (page 22) or Basic Brown Sauce (page 10), adding the liquid prepared earlier, from the livers, etc., also add cognac, lemon juice, salt and pepper. Bring to boil, then strain and add cream while reheating. Garnish with whipped potatoes and sauerkraut to which some white grapes and/or some champagne or dry white wine have been added. Instead of sauerkraut, Red Cabbage (page 67) can be substituted.

SUGGESTED WINES:
White Alsatian – Gewürztraminer
Red Bordeaux – Pomerol
Red Sparkling Burgundy

ROAST PHEASANT

A young male pheasant is usually preferable to a hen. After the bird has been killed, it is good to let it hang in a cool place for about 3 days in its feathers. It should never be allowed to hang for more than 4 or 5 days. A plump pheasant should be sufficient for 3 persons.
Clean well, and remove from cavity the heart, liver, stomach and cut of neck and set aside. Salt and pepper inside and out. Bard the breast completely with lard and bind with a thread. Brown bird on both sides, add consommé to about half the height of the bird, cover, and place in the oven, breast side down, for about 20 minutes at 350°F to 400°F. Remove lid, set bird on its back, and roast another 10 to 15 minutes. When cooked place on a large, fried crouton on a serving dish. During cooking, prepare one of the following sauces:
Take the heart, liver, stomach, and cut of neck. Chop them coarsely.

Sprinkle with cognac. Ignite and add consommé, enough to cover and simmer until reduced by half. Prepare 1½ cups of Game Sauce (page 22), add some of the liquid from the roasting pan and the liquid of the liver, heart, etc., and combine with game sauce and strain. Season to taste.

An alternate sauce could be a Basic Brown Sauce (page 10) to which cognac, a few drops of lemon juice and some liquid from the roasting pan and cream have been added as well as the liquid of the liver, heart, etc., combine with game sauce and strain. Served with sauerkraut, combined with some diced pineapple or white grapes heated, and/or a purée of chestnuts, or whipped potatoes.

SUGGESTED WINES:
Red Bordeaux (Claret) – Cos D'Estournel
Red Burgundy – Chambolle-Musigny
Red Burgundy – Clos de Vougeot
Red Sparkling Burgundy

STUFFED SQUAB MASCOTTE

For each person allow 1 plump squab. Clean well inside and out, then salt and pepper inside and out.

The following stuffing is sufficient for 6 squabs.

½ pound lard	3 to 5 chicken livers
½ pound lean pork meat	Chopped parsley
Livers from the squabs	12 medium-size mushrooms

Grind all ingredients together, then fry slowly for about 10 minutes over low heat. Stuff the cavities of the birds and sew up openings.

Place some butter in a heavy, flame-proof casserole, when hot, add squabs, also onions, carrots, parsley, and thyme. Brown squabs on all sides. Add half consommé and half dry red wine, enough to reach half the height of the birds. Bring to a boil, cover, and place in 350°F preheated oven. Simmer until tender. Remove the birds to serving platter and keep warm. Discard all vegetables.
To the liquid remaining in the pan, add 1 cup dry red wine, a little lemon juice, ½ cup Basic Brown Sauce (page 10) and for each squab, ½ tablespoon fresh butter. Boil until liquid is reduced to half, strain, and pour the sauce over the squabs.
Serve with French peas and noodles, rice, or parsley potatoes.

SUGGESTED WINES:
Red Bordeaux (Claret) – Saint Emilion
Red Rhône – Châteauneuf-du-Pape
Red Burgundy – Volnay

STUFFED TURKEY À L'ANCIENNE

Take a turkey of about 10 to 12 pounds, clean well inside and out, dampen the cavity with cognac. Push some thin slices of truffles under the skin of the breast and legs. Season with salt and pepper.

STUFFING:

Chop finely the turkey liver and about 10 chicken livers. Add ½ cup chopped onion, thyme, parsley, tarragon, and 1 cup chopped bacon. Sauté this mixture slightly in butter. Soak 10 slices white bread in milk, and squeeze out most of the milk. Add 3 egg yolks and 1 whole egg, salt, pepper, and 2 tablespoons cognac. Work this into the liver mixture well with your hands. Should the mixture prove to be too moist, add more bread crumbs until a satisfactory consistency is obtained. Taste for seasoning. Fill the cavity with the mixture and sew up the bird (also bind the neck with a string). Then brown the bird on all sides in butter in a roasting pan on top of the stove.

Fill the roasting pan about two thirds full with heated consommé. Place in a 450°F oven. Roast first on one side, then on the other, turning frequently until done. After the first hour, reduce the heat to about 300°F. During the last 30 minutes, place the bird on its back so that the breast is no longer in the liquid. Roasting time in the oven will take about 2½ to 3 hours or until done according to size of turkey.

Serve with Basic Brown Sauce (page 10) on the side, cranberries or Cumberland Sauce (page 21), Purée of Peas (page 70) or purée of, or whole, chestnuts, Brussels sprouts.

SUGGESTED WINES:
Red Bordeaux (Claret) – Saint Emilion
Red Rhône – Hermitage
Red Burgundy – Gevrey-Chambertin

meat

The meat course occupies
the most important place
in practically all menus. Therefore,
it should be selected and prepared
with special care.
The three major categories of meat
are red meat (beef and mutton),
white meat (veal), and
variety meats (liver, kidneys,
sweetbreads, and brains).

To add variety to menus and to avoid the possibility of serving the same main course more than once to a particular guest, one should explore the cuts and kinds of meat habitually prepared. The variety meats are frequently less expensive than other meats and provide especially valuable nutrients as well as an opportunity to display culinary ingenuity. About 5 to 7 oz. of meat exclusive of fat and bones should be allowed per person.
When a roast is on the menu, it should always be carved at the table in the old-fashioned manner. . . . Any roast is much more delicious when served in this way.

BOILED BEEF

To enjoy this dish it is important to buy the right cut. In most countries, even in most towns, butchers give it different names, but rump pot roast or hip of beef or, sometimes, the edge bone, also brisquet, are generally common. A piece of not less than 3 to 4 pounds is recommended.
Place beef in tepid water just to cover. Add salt, pepper, 1 well-washed leek, carrots, and onions. Cook to a boil, then lower heat and simmer for about 2 hours or until beef is tender. Some cubes of celery root, cabbage, carrots, and potatoes should be added during

the last 30 minutes of cooking. Boiled beef is served with all the vegetables that were cooked with it and, on the side, such things as sour pickles, beet salad, Horseradish Sauce (page 23) or Mayonnaise (page 15) mixed with a generous amount of chopped chives. The broth makes an excellent concentrated consommé that can be used in many dishes.

SUGGESTED WINES:
Red Bourdeaux – Château-Margaux
Red Beaujolais
Red Burgundy – Pommard

BEEF À LA MODE

To serve 5 to 6 persons, allow 3 to 4 pounds. Use the same cut of beef as in Boiled Beef (page 151) and should be larded by the butcher. In a heavy, flame-proof pan, heat a mixture of half butter and half oil with a few squares of salt pork. Toss in the bone of a veal knuckle (cracked), some sliced carrots, celery, a leek, and onions. Cook, stirring constantly, until all ingredients are well browned. Add beef, seasoned with salt and pepper, and brown on all sides. Pour in ½ cup dry red wine and enough consommé to reach half way up the meat. Add several skinned and sliced tomatoes, then cook to a boil. At this point cover and place in a preheated 325° F oven for 3 to 4 hours. Serve this dish, also called braised beef, with Basic Brown Sauce (page 10) to which a few drops of lemon juice and cognac or port have been added. Horseradish Sauce (page 23), noodles, or spaghetti, creamed spinach, and boiled potatoes are all traditional accompaniments.

TO SERVE COLD, which is excellent, place meat, after having prepared as above, in an earthenware paté dish. When completely cold, fill the dish to the brim with Aspic (page 8). Chill in refrigerator until firm. Serve with Cumberland Sauce (page 21) on the side.

SUGGESTED WINES:
Red Bordeaux (Claret) – Saint Estèphe
Red Rhône – Châteauneuf-du-Pape
Red Rhône – Hermitage
Red Burgundy – Gevrey-Chambertin

BEEF STROGANOFF

Only the filet of beef should be used for this dish. However, the point or tip of the filet can be used. Cut meat in strips about ½ inch thick and 2½ inches long. Heat some butter in a frying pan. When it is very hot, stir in beef and an ample amount of grated onion. Turn the mixture several times, then add some Basic Brown Sauce (page 10) and dry red wine (optional), sliced tomatoes, and sliced fresh mushrooms. Simmer about 10 minutes. Stir in some cognac and ignite. Add salt and pepper, chopped tarragon, julienne strips of cooked ham and some cream. Serve immediately.

SUGGESTED WINES:
Red Bordeaux (Claret) – Cos D'Estournel
Red Bordeaux (Claret) – Pomerol
Red Beaujolais

FILET OF BEEF EN CRÔUTE EPICURE

To serve 4 to 5 persons take 2 pounds of filet of beef cut from the center of a beef filet. Season with salt and pepper and either sauté or broil to the very rare stage. Let cool. Mix together equal amounts of finely chopped ham, chopped fresh mushrooms, and chopped, cooked spinach. Bind with a little Velouté (page 28), and season with salt, pepper and a dash of nutmeg. Press this mixture all around the cooled filet. Roll some puff paste about ⅛ of an inch thick and brush with beaten egg. Place filet on top and wrap pastry around the meat securely, enclosing meat completely. Brush the outside of the pastry on all sides with more beaten egg and make 2 little openings on top so that steam can escape. Decorate with small cutouts of puff paste and place on a greased baking sheet. Bake in a preheated 450° F oven until pastry is golden brown. When carved the meat will be beautifully pink and juicy. Beef en croûte should be accompanied by Basic Brown Sauce (page 10) to which a little sherry and some chopped truffles have been added.
NOTE: Enveloping the filet in the ham vegetable mixture helps to prevent the pastry from becoming soggy.

SUGGESTED WINES:
White Burgundy – Corton Charlemagne
Red Bordeaux (Claret) – Pauillac
Red Rhône – Côte Rotie

MEDAILLON OF BEEF MILO

Make some Sauce Mornay (page 25), heavy on the cheese, and stir in a little tomato purée. Keep warm while you fry small seasoned tournedos in hot butter until well-browned on both sides. Place beef on rounds of white bread, fried in butter. Pour sauce over all, sprinkle with grated cheese, and place under a preheated broiler to brown. Garnish serving dish with broiled tomatoes stuffed with a mixture of chopped olives, onions, and parsley.

SUGGESTED WINES:
Red Bordeaux (Claret) – Saint Emilion
Red Rhône – Côte Rotie
Red Beaujolais

BERNESE DISH (A COMBINATION OF BOILED MEATS)

Into a large kettle put a fresh calf's tongue, a piece of beef (same cut as for Boiled Beef, page 151) and smoked pork spareribs. Add enough water to cover and season with salt. Bring to a boil, reduce heat and simmer for about 1½ hours or until meats are almost tender. At this point add thick slices of cooked, smoked ham, frankfurters, and some peeled potatoes. Continue cooking until all meats are cooked through. In a separate saucepan cook some sauerkraut. When ready, place a large heap of sauerkraut on a serving platter and cover with the various meats, all sliced with the exception of the frankfurters. Surround with the potatoes and serve with Horseradish Sauce (page 23) and mustard.

SUGGESTED WINES:
White Alsatian – Gewürztraminer
White Loire – Pouilly-Fumé
Red Bordeaux (Claret) – Pomerol
Red Burgundy – Beaune

ENTRECÔTE WITH TARRAGON

Cook a little Basic Brown Sauce (page 10), with some dry red wine, ample tarragon leaves, consommé, salt and pepper until liquid is reduced to half. Broil a tender sirloin steak and serve sauce over it.

SUGGESTED WINES:
Red Bordeaux (Claret) – Saint Emilion
Red Burgundy – Nuits Saint Georges
Red Burgundy – Volnay

FILETS MIGNONS ALPHONSE

Combine some cooked spinach, cooked mushrooms and ham, all very finely chopped, and bind with a little Velouté (page 28). Broil or sauté very small filets mignons the way you like them. Fill medium-size vol-au-vents with the hot spinach mixture, top each with a filet mignon. On one half of the filet spoon some Madeira Sauce (page 24); on the other, Sauce Béarnaise (page 19). Serve immediately.

Garnish the serving platters with small heaps of diced cooked carrots, diced French fried potatoes and green peas and/or stringbeans.

SUGGESTED WINES:
Red Bordeaux (Claret) – Pomerol
Red Rhône – Côte Rotie
Red Burgundy – Chambolle-Musigny

FILETS MIGNONS HENRY IV

Make some Sauce Béarnaise (page 19), spoon into a pastry bag, and refrigerate until almost firm.

Broil seasoned filets mignons and when done to your taste, press a ½-inch edging of sauce around each filet. Dip a large, lightly sautéed mushroom cap in finely chopped parsley and place in center of each filet. Serve with asparagus tips and French fried potatoes.

SUGGESTED WINES:
White Burgundy – Musigny
Red Bordeaux (Claret) – Saint Estèphe
Red Rhône – Hermitage

FILETS MIGNONS MOSCOVITE

Take small filets mignons, sauté them in butter or broil. Remove from pan, top each with a thin slice of lemon spread with about ½ tablespoon caviar. On the side serve Mayonnaise (page 15) into which an ample amount of fresh horseradish has been mixed. Garnish with shoestring potatoes and broiled tomatoes are excellent accompaniments.

SUGGESTED WINES:
White Burgundy — Corton Charlemagne
Red Bordeaux (Claret) —Saint Estèphe
Red Sparkling Burgundy

FILETS MIGNONS PORTUGAISE

Blend together some Basic Brown Sauce (page 10) with a little dry white wine, an ample amount of tomato purée, salt and pepper. Keep hot while you sauté seasoned filets mignons to your taste. Garnish each filet with 4 anchovy filets, crosswise, pour the sauce over the meat and place a stuffed olive on top.
Serve with Ratatouille (page 47).

SUGGESTED WINES:
Red Rhône — Châteauneuf-du-Pape
Red Rhône — Hermitage
Red Burgundy — Chambolle-Musigny

GOULASH TYROLIENNE

For 4 persons take 2 pounds of beef (same cut as for Boiled Beef, page 151) and cut into 2 inch squares. Put 2 tablespoons butter, 1 tablespoon oil and 3 large onions sliced in a heavy kettle. Add beef cubes, which first have been sprinkled with flour and seasoned with salt and pepper. Brown well. Cover with half consommé and half Basic Brown Sauce (page 10) and bring to a boil. Add 6 large tomatoes sliced. Cover and simmer for 2 to 3 hours or until beef is tender. Before serving, stir in a little tomato purée, some cream, and thicken with a few pieces of Beurre Manié (page 10). Sprinkle with chopped parsley.

SUGGESTED WINES:
Red Bordeaux (Claret) – Château-Margaux
Red Burgundy – Beaune
Red Burgundy – Gevrey-Chambertin

MEAT ON A SKEWER À LA TURQUE

Good combination of flavors: Small pieces of beef filet about 1 inch square, pieces of bacon, small onions and tomatoes, chicken livers, veal or lamb kidneys, and mushrooms. Try to have all the component foods approximately the same size. Thread on a skewer alternately. Sprinkle with salt and pepper. Brush with oil, then coat in fine bread crumbs. Broil in a preheated broiler, turning skewers occasionally, until crisp and well browned. Serve Steak Sauce (page 26) and rice on the side.

SUGGESTED WINES:
Red Bordeaux (Claret) – Saint Estèphe
Red Rhône – Châteauneuf-du-Pape
Red Burgundy – Chambolle-Musigny

MINUTE STEAK PROVENÇALE

Cut a sirloin steak ½ to ¾ inch thick, salt and pepper. Melt some butter and pour half of the hot butter over the steak. Let rest for 30 minutes. Then sauté the steak. For each steak, chop ½ medium-size onion finely, and combine with 1 teaspoon French mustard, and ¼ cup dry white wine. Bring to boil and reduce to half. Add chopped parsley and pour this sauce over the steak.

SUGGESTED WINES:
Red Bordeaux (Claret) – Saint Estèphe
Red Rhône – Châteauneuf-du-Pape
Red Burgundy – Chambolle-Musigny

STEAK DU BARRY

Sauté filets mignons, place a poached egg on top of each and cover with Madeira Sauce (page 24).

SUGGESTED WINES:
Red Bordeaux (Claret) – Pauillac
Red Burgundy – Gevrey-Chambertin
Red Burgundy – Pommard

STEAK AU POIVRE VENDÔME

Choose filets mignons or a thick sirloin. Salt, then press a generous amount of freshly crushed black pepper into both sides of the meat. Heat butter in a skillet. When very hot, add meat and sauté on both sides. Remove beef to a heated serving platter. Stir in a little Basic Brown Sauce (page 10), a lump of butter and some dry sherry into the skillet. Heat and pour over the beef.

SUGGESTED WINES:
Red Bordeaux (Claret) – Saint Estèphe
Red Rhône – Châteauneuf-du-Pape
Red Burgundy – Chambolle-Musigny

TOURNEDOS ALBERT

Sauté small, seasoned tournedos in very hot butter. While they cook, pour a little port wine over them. When almost done, stir in some Basic Brown Sauce (page 10), cream, salt and pepper, lightly sautéed mushroom slices and, if necessary, more port. Serve tournedos in the sauce with shoestring potatoes on the side.

SUGGESTED WINES:
Red Bordeaux (Claret) – Saint Julien
Red Burgundy – Pommard
Red Burgundy – Vosne-Romanée

HAM À L'ANCIENNE (STUFFED HAM)

This is an excellent, old-fashioned dish for a dinner party. You need a well-cured, mild ham of not less than 10 pounds, the larger the better.

Soak ham overnight in cold water, if the ham requires it (this is necessary with some Southern or Virginia hams). Drain, cover with fresh water, and simmer until tender. Remove from liquid and trim off as much fat as possible. Now cut the largest possible square out of the center of the ham, leaving only a thin wall of meat remaining on bottom and sides. Cut this piece into thin, neat slices, place on a platter and cover with a little boiling consommé to keep meat hot and moist. Place the whole ham on serving platter. While ham is cooking make the following sauce and stuffing: Cut 2 cooked and skinned sweetbreads in ½ inch cubes. Take approximately the same size and quantity of mushrooms (optional: coarsely chopped truffles) and sauté lightly in a little butter. Make some Chicken Forcemeat (page 13) and mold with a teaspoon to make ovals (quenelles). Now make a Velouté (page 28) with consommé. Stir in a little dry white wine and cream. Combine half the heated sauce with sweetbreads, mushrooms, chicken quenelles (diced white meat of

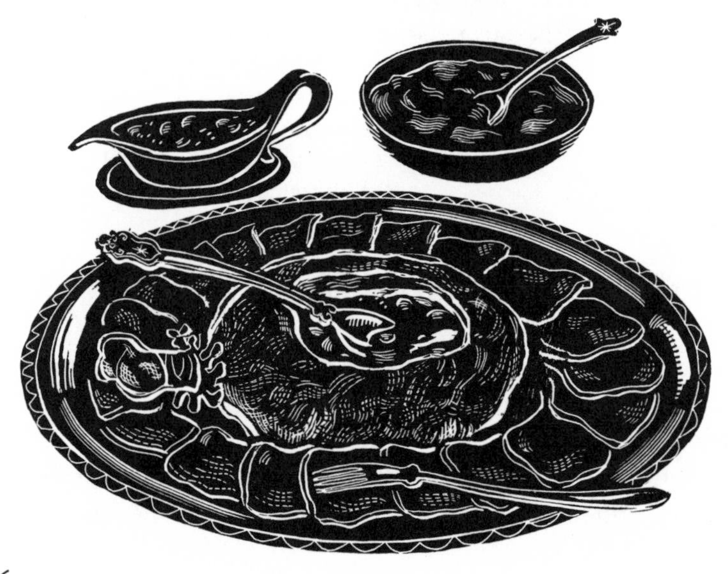

chicken can be used in place of quenelles), and the chopped truffles. Spoon into ham cavity. (See to it that the sauce is thin.) Serve remaining sauce containing more of the filling on the side. Arrange slices of ham taken from the center overlapping around the base of the ham. Serve hot with Madeira Sauce (page 24), creamed spinach, and fine noodles.

SUGGESTED WINES:
White Rhine (Hock) – Riesling
White Bordeaux – Graves
White Bordeaux – Margaux
Red Rhône – Tavel

HAM MEXICAN STYLE

Take a mildly-cured ham of about 6 to 8 pounds, cover with cold water, bring to boil, and simmer for 2½ hours at 350° F. Skin ham, taking off most of the fat, leaving only a thin surrounding layer. Make a few crosswise incisions into the fat, sprinkle lavishly with sugar, place in hot oven, baste every 5 to 10 minutes with half dry white wine and half sherry. After about 1 hour remove ham and keep warm. Reduce liquid remaining in the pan by about half, add an equal amount of Basic Brown Sauce (page 10), season with salt and pepper, and thicken if necessary with Beurre Manié (page 10). Serve the sauce on the side with a Purée of French Peas (page 70).

SUGGESTED WINES:
White Burgundy – Meursault
Red Bordeaux (Claret) – Pomerol
Red Rhône – Tavel

SADDLE OF HARE

The saddle of a young hare will serve about 3 persons. Skin well and remove sinews. Salt and pepper and sprinkle with paprika. Pour melted butter over the hare and let stand for 1 hour.

Heat butter, add ½ cup each diced bacon and sliced onion to roasting pan. Add hare. Place in preheated hot oven and baste frequently with sour cream. The roast should be done after 25 to 35 minutes at about 400° F. Serve with Game Sauce (page 22) on the side, Red Cabbage (page 67), and noodles.

SUGGESTED WINES:
Red Bordeaux – Saint Estèphe
Red Rhône – Côte Rotie
Red Burgundy – Chambolle-Musigny

STEW OF HARE PROVENÇALE

Wash, skin, and take out sinews of hare, cut in fairly large chunks. Place overnight in refrigerator in the following marinade: Onion rings, pepper, salt, sliced carrots, bay leaf, thyme, garlic, and enough water and vinegar, half and half, to cover. Next day dry meat well with a cloth and turn each piece in flour. Place in ovenproof casserole ½ cup diced bacon, ½ cup butter. When very hot, add meat and turn several times. Then add 2 to 3 cups of the marinade, ½ bottle dry red wine, 1 cup Basic Brown Sauce (page 10), 2 tablespoons cognac and 2 tablespoons red currant jelly. Bring to boil, cover, simmer in oven of 350° F for 2 hours. Then add 2 cups coarsely chopped mushrooms, and about 20 small white onions, continue cooking until vegetables are tender. (Optional: ¼ cup of the blood of the hare mixed with the juice of 1 lemon). Serve with mashed potatoes and Red Cabbage (page 67). Serves 4 to 6 persons.

SUGGESTED WINES:
White Beaujolais – Moulin-à-Vent
Red Bordeaux (Claret) – Saint Estèphe
Red Rhône – Hermitage
Red Rhône – Tavel

KIDNEYS GRAND DUKE

Trim lamb or veal kidneys and sauté in butter until done. Place on slices of white bread fried in butter in a serving dish. Fill each with Sauce Béarnaise (page 19) and garnish with lightly sautéed mushroom caps. Serve with shoestring potatoes.

SUGGESTED WINES:
White Burgundy – Clos de Vougeot
White Burgundy – Corton Charlemagne
Red Bordeaux (Claret) – Saint Emilion

VEAL KIDNEYS MADEIRA

Place skinned, cleaned kidneys in cold water for 30 minutes. Dry and slice kidneys. Place in skillet with hot butter, add grated onion and cook over slow fire. When done, add Basic Brown Sauce (page

10), Madeira wine, chopped parsley and tarragon, salt, and pepper. Lamb kidneys can be substituted for veal kidneys.

SUGGESTED WINES:
White Burgundy – Corton Charlemagne
Red Bordeaux (Claret) – Pomerol
Red Burgundy – Chambolle-Musigny

CURRY OF LAMB INDIENNE

Prepare like Curry of Veal (page 176).

SUGGESTED WINES:
White Rhine (Hock) – Liebfraumilch
White Burgundy – Pouilly-Fuissé
Red Bordeaux (Claret) – Pomerol

LAMB CHOPS MORNAY

Broil or sauté lamb chops. Salt and pepper. Remove from pan, sprinkle with grated cheese, then top with Sauce Mornay (page 25). Sprinkle again with cheese and a few drops of melted butter. Set under the broiler to brown. Serve with potato chips and green beans.

SUGGESTED WINES:
Red Bordeaux (Claret) – Pauillac
Red Burgundy – Beaune
Red Burgundy – Nuits Saint George

SADDLE OF LAMB HERMITAGE

Same as Saddle of Veal (page 174).

SUGGESTED WINES:
Red Bordeaux (Claret) – Pomerol
Red Bordeaux – Saint Emilion
Red Rhône – Tavel
Red Burgundy – Vosne-Romanée

CALF'S BRAINS IN BLACK BUTTER

Cook very fresh calf's brains in salted water. Remove membrane and slice about 1½ inches thick. Pat dry, place in a serving dish and keep warm. Place a generous amount of butter in a saucepan, add a little chopped onion and heat until butter is almost black and giving off a nut-like fragrance. Sprinkle calf's brains with an ample amount of well-drained capers, a little lemon juice and pour on the hot black butter over all. Serve immediately.

SUGGESTED WINES:
White Burgundy – Meursault
Red Bordeaux (Claret) – Pomerol
Red Burgundy – Beaune

CALF'S LIVER, ENGLISH STYLE

Skin and cut very fresh, light-colored calf's liver as thick as you like. Remove all membrane and dust the slices with flour. Sauté both sides quickly in heated butter. Sprinkle with salt and pepper and serve with crisp bacon and/or fried onion rings.

SUGGESTED WINES:
Red Bordeaux (Claret) – Saint Julien
Red Burgundy – Gevrey-Chambertin

CALF'S LIVER, SWISS STYLE

Take a very fresh calf's liver and skin. Slice to about ⅛ inch thick and ¼ inch wide. Turn in flour. Heat butter in a pan, add sliced onion rings, brown slightly, then add the liver, a little dry white wine, and Basic Brown Sauce (page 10) to cover. Place lid on top and simmer for about 5 minutes. Season with salt and pepper. Serve liver in its sauce.

SUGGESTED WINES:
White Burgundy – Puligny-Montrachet
Red Bordeaux (Claret) – Saint Emilion
Red Beaujolais

CALF'S LIVER TYROLIENNE

Skin and slice very fresh calf's liver about ¼ inch thick, turn in flour, sauté in butter, then remove the liver and keep warm. In the same saucepan sauté some sliced onion rings turned in flour, add more butter, salt, and pepper. When onions are tender, add drained capers, cream, and lemon juice. Stir well and pour over calf's liver.

SUGGESTED WINES:
White Rhine (Hock) – Riesling
White Bordeaux – Margaux
Red Burgundy – Volnay

MIXED GRILL, ORIENTAL STYLE

To serve 4 take 4 Chipolata sausages, 4 well-cleaned lamb kidneys, 4 small and thinly cut slices of calf's liver, 1 calf's brain sliced in 4, 4 very small pieces of filet of beef. Broil all together. Sauté in butter, after having turned in flour and slightly beaten egg white: 2 peeled and sliced bananas, 2 peeled and sliced eggplants, 4 thin slices of melon and 4 thin slices of pineapple. Serve with curried rice and broiled tomatoes on the side.

SUGGESTED WINES:
White Rhine (Hock) – Riesling
White Rhône – Hermitage
Red Rhône – Tavel
Red Burgundy – Volnay

FILET OF PORK EN CRÔUTE BRISTOL

Prepare as for Filet of Beef en Croûte Epicure (page 154). Use meat from liver sausage (instead of spinach combination) to cover the filet before enveloping it in puff paste.

SUGGESTED WINES:
White Burgundy – Corton Charlemagne
Red Bordeaux (Claret) – Pomerol
Red Rhône – Tavel

SWEETBREADS MASCOTTE

Allow a whole sweetbread for each person and poach in salted water. When cooked, remove membrane and dry the sweetbreads thoroughly. Sauté in butter with some grated onion until golden. Sprinkle with a little grated Gruyère cheese and place under a preheated broiler until cheese takes on a good color. Remove to a serving dish and keep warm. Make a Velouté (page 28) with mushroom stock and stir in slices of lightly sautéed mushrooms, some more grated Gruyère, some cream mixed with 1 egg yolk. Then add a dash of port wine and a little Basic Brown Sauce (page 10) to step up the flavor. Pour sauce over sweetbreads.

SUGGESTED WINES:
White Bordeaux – Graves
White Bordeaux – Margaux
White Burgundy – Pouilly-Fuissé

OSSO BUCO NIÇOISE

Have veal knuckles split in half if they look too large for one serving. Dip knuckles in beaten egg, season with salt and pepper, then coat with flour. Fry in heated oil until brown on all sides. Remove from pan and set aside for the moment. Add chopped bacon to pan and cook until almost crisp. Stir in a large onion, sliced, some sliced mushrooms, and tomatoes cut in dice. Return meat to pan and add chopped parsley, a little rind of orange cut in julienne, diced carrots, peas, consommé and some tomato purée. Cover tightly and simmer for 1 to 1½ hours or until veal is very tender. Serve with its own juice and vegetables and spaghetti.

SUGGESTED WINES:
White Rhône – Hermitage
White Verdicchio – Castelli di Jesi
Red Bordeaux (Claret) – Pomerol
Red Rhône – Châteauneuf-du-Pape

SCHNITZEL À LA HOLSTEIN

Have veal cutlets cut about ½-inch thick (remove bone if any). Pound until thin, then season with salt and pepper. Coat with flour, dip in beaten egg, then cover with fine bread crumbs. Heat a mixture of half butter and half oil in a frying pan. When very hot, add cutlets and sauté both sides until well browned. Place a fried egg on top of each cutlet, sprinkle with red pepper and cross 2 anchovy filets on top. Garnish with chopped parsley on one side of the egg, well-drained capers on the other. Serve with Lyonnaise potatoes.

SUGGESTED WINES:
White Burgundy – Meursault
Red Bordeaux (Claret) – Saint Emilion
Red Burgundy – Pommard

BITOTSCHKIS OF VEAL

For 6 to 8 persons take 1 pound ground veal, 1 pound ground pork, 2 slices ground calf's liver, ½ pound bacon and 3 slices white bread, crusts removed. Work all together through the finest blade of meat grinder. Blend thoroughly with 2 eggs plus 1 extra yolk, some grated onion, salt, and pepper. Shape into small patties about 1¼ inches in diameter and about ½ inch thick. Turn in flour. Heat a mixture of 3 tablespoons butter and 2 tablespoons oil in a skillet. When very hot, fry meat patties on both sides. Serve with some creamed Basic Brown Sauce (page 10) combined with a little tomato purée, sliced and lightly sautéed mushrooms. Bitotschkis of veal is good with rice, spaghetti, or noodles and creamed spinach.

SUGGESTED WINES:
White Burgundy – Puligny-Montrachet
Red Bordeaux (Claret) – Saint Emilion
Red Burgundy – Volnay

GESCHNAETZELTES OF VEAL

This is a well known Swiss dish.
For 4 to 5 persons buy about 1½ pounds young veal, preferably from the filet, and shave off slices about ⅛ of an inch thick. Heat 2 tablespoons butter in a saucepan. When very hot, add veal, sprinkle lightly with flour, salt, and pepper. Cook over a high heat for 5 minutes, stirring constantly. At this point, the meat is done. Stir in some grated onion, a bit of tomato juice (optional: dry white wine) ½ cup of Basic Brown Sauce (page 10) and 1 cup heavy cream. Reheat, do not boil. Serve with rice, noodles, spaghetti, or Spaetzle (page 100).

SUGGESTED WINES:
White Burgundy – Puligny-Montrachet
White Swiss – Neuchâtel
Red Bordeaux (Claret) – Saint Julien

VEAL MILANAISE

Take about 2 to 3 pound leg of veal, tied securely. In a heavy casserole heat 2 tablespoons butter with 2 tablespoons oil, chopped veal bones, and a grated onion. When fat is very hot, add veal and brown on all sides over a high heat. Pour in a mixture of half Basic Brown

Sauce (page 10) and half consommé, enough to reach halfway up the meat. Roast, uncovered, in a preheated 425° F hot oven for 1 to 1¼ hours, basting frequently with the pan juices. During the last 30 minutes add ample skinned and sliced tomatoes. Before serving take out bones, sprinkle the top lavishly with grated Parmesan cheese and broil until cheese is golden. Serve with basic brown sauce on the side.

SUGGESTED WINES:
White Rhône – Hermitage
Red Bordeaux (Claret) – Saint Julien
Red Burgundy – Volnay

PAPRIKA VEAL CUTLETS

For 4 persons take 4 veal cutlets flattened to a thickness of about ¼ inch, turn in flour. Heat butter in a pan, add a few drops of oil, chopped onions, ample paprika, and stir quickly. Then add the veal cutlets and brown on both sides. When tender add a little lemon juice, ample sour cream and more paprika. Serve with Spaetzle (page 100), noodles, or rice.

SUGGESTED WINES:
White Rhine (Hock) – Liebfraumilch
White Burgundy – Pouilly-Fuissé
Red Bordeaux (Claret) – Pomerol

PAPRIKA GOULASH OF VEAL

For 4 persons cut 2 pounds of veal (the best meat is from the leg) into 2 inch cubes. Heat 2 tablespoons butter and 1 tablespoon oil in a heavy kettle and add some coarsely chopped onions. When fat is very hot, add veal, having sprinkled it with salt, pepper, and flour. Brown on all sides. Add a generous amount of paprika. Add 2 or 3 large onions, sliced, 2 to 3 tablespoons Basic Brown Sauce (page 10) and enough consommé to almost cover. Cook to a boil, place lid on top, then reduce heat and simmer about 1½ hours or until tender. Make a small amount of Velouté (page 28), add a generous amount of paprika, and stir in part of the liquid in which the veal cooked. Add some dry white wine (optional), cream, the cubes of cooked veal, and chopped parsley. Simmer another 20 minutes. This same paprika goulash can be made with cubes of lean beef in place of the veal.

SUGGESTED WINES:
White Rhine (Hock) – Rüdesheimer
Red Bordeaux (Claret) – Pomerol
Red Rhône – Hermitage

SADDLE OF VEAL HERMITAGE

Have your butcher cut a large saddle of veal. In a heavy flame-proof casserole large enough to contain the meat, heat a mixture of half butter and half oil. Add some sliced onions and carrots and brown well. Season veal with salt and pepper. Add to casserole and brown on all sides. Pour in consommé, enough to reach halfway up the sides of the meat, cover with a lid and simmer in a preheated 350° F to 400° F oven until well done. While veal cooks prepare the following sauce: Make a Velouté (page 28) with consommé or mushroom stock. Add some dry white wine, salt, pepper, grated onion, and a little tomato purée. Then stir in cream mixed with egg yolks. Make the sauce rather thin.

Carve the cooked saddle lengthwise, following the bone, then cut it diagonally in slices about 2- to 2½-inches wide. Moisten the cavity on both sides of the saddle with the sauce and reset the carved slices on the saddle, placing a thick layer of lightly sautéed mushrooms and sliced truffles between each piece of meat. To the remaining sauce add some grated Parmesan and Gruyère cheese, also a little Basic Brown Sauce (page 10) and egg yolks. Mix well and cover entire saddle with this sauce. Sprinkle with more grated cheese and place under a preheated broiler to brown.

Serve with Dauphine Potatoes (page 71), French peas, and Tarragon Sauce (page 26) on the side.

SUGGESTED WINES:
White Burgundy — Clos de Vougeot
White Burgundy — Meursault
Red Bordeaux (Claret) — Saint Emilion

STUFFED VEAL STEAK MIRABEAU

Allow 1 veal cutlet per person. Remove bone if any. Pound veal slightly to flatten and season with salt and pepper. Sauté in butter with a little grated onion until both sides are nicely browned. Chop a cooked calf's brain or a sweetbread extremely fine and mix with chopped parsley, salt, pepper, cream mixed with 1 egg yolk, and a little grated Parmesan cheese. Spread some of the mixture on each veal cutlet, sprinkle with more chopped parsley and grated Parmesan. Place under a preheated broiler to brown slightly.

SUGGESTED WINES:
White Bordeaux — Margaux
White Burgundy — Montrachet
White Burgundy — Pouilly-Fuissé

BLANQUETTE DE VEAU À L'ANCIENNE

For 4 to 5 persons cut 1½ to 2 pounds veal in 1½-inch cubes and season with salt and pepper. Heat 2 or 3 tablespoons butter in a flame proof pan. When hot stir in same amount of chopped onion. When onion begins to take on color, add veal and cook over a high heat, stirring frequently, until lightly browned. Pour in enough consommé to cover veal, bring to a boil, then cover with lid, reduce heat and simmer for 1 to 1½ hours or until meat is tender.
Make a Velouté (page 28) with consommé or mushroom stock. Stir in strained liquid from veal, veal cubes, some small cooked onions, lightly sautéed mushroom slices (optional), and 1 cup of cream mixed with 2 egg yolks. Simmer a few minutes longer but do

not boil. This dish can also be made with lamb. As a variation you can substitute Curry Sauce (page 22) for the Velouté.

SUGGESTED WINES:
White Rhine (Hock) – Riesling
White Burgundy – Pouilly-Fuissé
Red Bordeaux (Claret) – Pomerol

SADDLE OF VENISON

A whole saddle of a young animal should be sufficient for about 8 to 10 people. Before dressing, hang the animal for 3 to 4 days in a cool place. Skin, and take out sinews, then salt and pepper. (Larding the saddle is optional). Combine butter, onions, carrots, thyme, and bay leaf in roasting pan and place on top of stove to take on color. Add the venison, place in hot 450° F oven and baste frequently with heavy cream. The roast should be done in about 40 minutes unless it is preferred rare. Make Game Sauce (page 22), adding some liquid from the roasting pan. Season to taste or use creamed Basic Brown Sauce (page 10) to which lemon juice, 1 egg yolk, and a little cognac have been added. Serve with sautéed mushrooms and/or sauerkraut or Red Cabbage (page 67), mashed potatoes, or chestnuts.

SUGGESTED WINES:
White Burgundy – Musigny
Red Bordeaux (Claret) – Saint Estèphe
Red Rhône – Hermitage
Red Sparkling Burgundy

Brandy

chafing dishes

Cooking at the table over a chafing dish has become increasingly popular in recent years. Preparing eggs, fowls, meat, fish, or dessert dishes at the table is not difficult; but it should be used as a means of food preparation *only when* it is justified for strictly culinary reasons —not, as is often the case, as an opportunity to show off to one's guests.
The recipes in this chapter have been carefully selected as especially appropriate for preparation at the table. This is a sociable, informal means of cooking, ideal for the host who has no help which makes it possible to serve the dishes at exactly the right moment.
All of the necessary ingredients should be prepared in advance and waiting in the kitchen. Then they may be brought into the dining room conveniently at the appropriate time. Cooking time of all the chafing dishes is comparatively brief; the speed of transfer from chafing dish to individual plate enhances the flavor of these specialties. Just as a roast is most delicious when *carved* at the table, these recipes are for foods which are best *prepared* at the table.

CHERRIES JUBILEE

Place in individual containers: Butter, sugar, julienne of lemon and orange rind, orange juice, red currant or raspberry jelly, pitted dessert cherries, cherry brandy, kirsch, vanilla ice cream, blanched almonds, toasted and slivered.

In chafing dish pan melt butter, add plenty of sugar as well as lemon and orange rind, cook until mixture starts to stick to the pan, but do not brown. Stir in orange juice, red currant or raspberry jelly, and cherries. Simmer about 5 to 10 minutes. While still simmering, add cherry brandy, remove lemon and orange rind, and add kirsch. Ignite. Place a serving of vanilla ice cream on dessert plates, spoon some of the cherries and their sauce over the serving. Sprinkle top with almonds.

SUGGESTED WINES:
Asti – Spumante
Champagne

STUFFED BABY CHICKEN OR SQUAB ROYAL

Cook some rice, drain, and mix with a little chopped onion, chopped raw chicken livers and parsley, salt and pepper. Stuff cavities of baby chickens or squab with mixture, roast until tender, then arrange on a serving dish. Keep warm. Place in individual containers: Cognac, butter, chopped onion, Basic Brown Sauce (page 10), port wine, cream, salt, pepper, and lemon juice. In chafing dish pan heat some butter, stir in chopped onion, salt and freshly ground pepper. Add basic brown sauce, port wine, and enough heavy cream to make a good sauce consistency, adding a few drops of lemon juice. Sprinkle chickens or squabs with cognac and ignite. Split birds, if desired, in half. Pour hot sauce over them. Serve with green beans or creamed spinach, shoestring potatoes.

SUGGESTED WINES:
White Loire – Pouilly-Fumé
White Burgundy – Clos des Mouches
White Orvieto – Secco

CHICKEN NORMANDE

Take a young chicken and cut in four, salt and pepper. Sauté in butter until tender. Place in serving dish and keep warm. Bring to your chafing dish table: Butter, 1½ cups heavy cream mixed with 2 egg yolks and calvados.
Melt a little butter in the chafing dish then mix in the cream-egg yolk mixture, taste for seasoning. Sprinkle the chicken lavishly with calvados, ignite, then pour the sauce over the chicken. Serve with fresh green beans.

SUGGESTED WINES:
White Moselle – Bernkastel
White Burgundy – Clos de Vougeot
White – Soave

CRÈPES DUCHESSE WITH BERRIES

Place in individual containers: Crêpes (page 11) made slightly larger than in basic recipe, butter, sugar, fresh strawberries and/or raspberries (or frozen berries), an orange base liqueur such as, Grand Marnier, Bénédictine, Cointreau, kirsch or cognac.
In chafing dish pan, melt butter and some sugar. Heat the crêpes in this mixture. While the crêpes are heating, mash fruits lightly with a fork, sprinkle with a bit of sugar, and marinate in equal parts of Grand Marnier and cognac, for example. Fill each crêpe generously with the marinated berry mixture, then fold over once, sprinkle with sugar, add kirsch or cognac and ignite. Serve immediately.

SUGGESTED WINES:
Asti – Spumante
Champagne

CRÊPES JEANNETTE

Place in individual containers: Crêpes (page 11), butter, orange marmalade, julienne of orange rind, confectioners sugar, orange juice, arrack or cognac.
In chafing dish melt butter, stir in some orange marmalade, orange rind and sugar. When well blended, add orange juice. Bathe all crêpes on both sides with the mixture, fold like a handkerchief, add warmed arrack or cognac and ignite.

SUGGESTED WINES:
Asti – Spumante
Champagne

CRÊPES OTHELLO

Make Crêpes (page 11). For each crêpe take 1 tablespoon Crème Pâtissière (page 18), mix with Grand Marnier, spread on crêpes, fold over once. Place ample butter in chafing dish. When hot, add the crêpes, sprinkle with toasted split almonds, confectioners' sugar and cognac. Ignite and serve.

SUGGESTED WINES:
White Burgundy – Chablis
White Bordeaux – Graves
Asti – Spumante
Champagne

SCRAMBLED EGGS WINDSOR

(See page 84).

FILET MIGNON WITH MUSHROOMS

Place in individual containers: Sauce Bordelaise (page 19) cream, small, cooked whole mushrooms, bay leaf, chopped parsley and tarragon, cognac, lemon juice, salt, pepper, and the filets mignons, cognac, and cream. Season filets with salt and pepper and sauté in well-heated butter. In another pan, heat sauce Bordelaise and all the ingredients *except cognac and cream.* Remove pan from flame for the moment. Now heat cognac in a ladle and ignite. Return sauce to flame, pour in flaming cognac, stir in cream, and taste for seasoning. Pour over filets and serve immediately.
Garnish with shoestring potatoes and stringbeans.

SUGGESTED WINES:
Red Bordeaux (Claret) – Médoc
Red Bordeaux (Claret) – Pomerol
Red Bordeaux (Claret) – Saint Julien

FONDUE BOURGUIGNONNE

Bring to table cubes of filet mignon about ¾-inch square and the following: Mayonnaise (page 15) seasoned with plenty of French mustard, Special Cocktail Sauce (page 21), finely chopped avocado mixed with chopped onion, chile, fresh tomato, Russian Salad (page 52), green onions, anchovy filets, sour pickles, hot Steak Sauce (page 26). Pour enough vegetable oil into a heavy, fairly deep, small saucepan to fill to a depth of ½ to ¾ capacity. Heat to sizzling. The easiest way to determine if the correct temperature has been obtained is to place a wooden spoon in the oil. When the oil sizzles around the spoon and forms small blisters, the right temperature for frying the meat has been reached. Place a cube of beef on a long, thin fork or wooden stick, plunge meat into the hot oil and brown to your taste. Dip into the sauce of your choice before eating. Special equipment for preparing fondues (both cheese and Bourguignonne) are available in most stores carrying imported cooking equipment.

SUGGESTED WINES:
White Beaujolais – Moulin-à-Vent
Red Bordeaux (Claret) – Pomerol
Red Bordeaux (Claret) – Saint Emilion

GOULASH À LA MINUTE

For 2 to 3 portions take ¾ to 1 pound filet of beef, slice about ¼ of an inch thick and 1 to 1¼ inches wide. Season with salt and pepper. Bring to chafing dish table the following: Butter and cream, 2 tablespoons chopped onion, chopped parsley, tarragon, the raw meat, cognac, ½ cup stock, ½ cup Basic Brown Sauce (page 10), ½ cup cooked peas.
Place 2 tablespoons of butter in chafing dish pan, add onion, parsley, tarragon. When butter starts to smoke, add the meat, stir quickly, add ½ tablespoon cognac, ignite, then add stock, the basic brown sauce, peas, and cook a few minutes (optional: cream). Serve with rice or boiled potatoes on the side.

SUGGESTED WINES:
Red Bordeaux (Claret) – Saint Emilion
Red Rhône – Châteauneuf-du-Pape
Red Beaujolais
Red Chianti

GUINEA HEN FLAMBÉ DU BARRY

Stuff guinea hen with rice stuffing (see Stuffed Baby Chicken or Squab, page 146), or wild rice. Roast in oven until done. Place in individual containers: Butter, Basic Brown Sauce (page 10), red currant jelly, salt and pepper, chopped thyme and parsley, cream, lemon juice, cognac. In chafing dish heat very little butter, add basic brown sauce, red currant jelly, salt, plenty of freshly ground pepper, chopped thyme, and parsley. Stir until jelly has dissolved, then add cream, a little lemon juice.
Pour heated cognac over the hot guinea hen and ignite.
Let burn a moment, then pour sauce over bird.

SUGGESTED WINES:
White Bordeaux – Graves
White Burgundy – Corton Charlemagne
White Burgundy – Macon

KIDNEYS FLAMBÉ ROUENNAISE

Place in individual containers: Butter, skinned and trimmed, sliced lamb or veal kidneys, onion, salt and pepper, cognac, canned pureé of foie gras or Mousse of Duck (page 38), Basic Brown Sauce (page 10), chopped parsley, and cream. Melt butter in chafing dish. When sizzling hot, add kidneys, onion, salt, and pepper. Cook kidneys until done to your taste, sprinkle with cognac and ignite. When flame dies away, lift kidneys out of pan and set aside. Stir pureé of foie gras or mousse of duck into liquid remaining in chafing dish pan, adding basic brown sauce, parsley, and cream. Mix well, replace kidneys, spoon sauce over the kidneys, heat through and serve.

SUGGESTED WINES:
Red Rhône – Châteauneuf-du-Pape
Red Rhône – Hermitage
Red Chianti

CALF'S LIVER TIVOLI

For 4 persons take 10 thin slices ¼ inch thick of very fresh calf's liver, cut into strips ½ inch wide and 2 inches long. Turn in flour. Bring the following ingredients to the chafing dish table: Butter, chopped onion, calf's liver, chopped parsley, Basic Brown Sauce (page 10), sherry, salt, pepper, stock.
Place ample butter in pan with chopped onion. When butter starts to smoke, add calf's liver and stir quickly until browned. Add parsley, ½ cup of stock, 4 tablespoons basic brown sauce and 1 to 1½ tablespoons sherry, salt and pepper. Serve liver in its sauce with Lyonnaise potatoes and buttered peas.

SUGGESTED WINES:
Red Bordeaux – Médoc
Red Beaujolais
Red Valpolicella

SALMIS OF LOBSTER CÔTE D'AZUR

Place in individual containers: Lobster Butter (page 14), Sauce Américaine (page 18), chopped parsley, salt, pepper, meat of a

cooked lobster in bite-size pieces, lightly sautéed mushrooms, cognac, cream.
In chafing dish, heat a little of the lobster butter, stir in sauce américaine, the parsley, salt, and freshly ground pepper. Mix in lobster meat and mushrooms. Remove pan from the flame. Pour some cognac in a small ladle, heat and ignite. Replace the chafing dish over the flame, stir in the cognac, add sufficient cream to achieve the right consistency. Taste for seasoning. Serve with rice on the side.

SUGGESTED WINES:
White Rhine (Hock) – Rüdesheimer
White Bordeaux – Graves
White – Soave

FLAMED OMELETTE WITH APPLES

Place in individual containers: Butter, 6 to 8 eggs beaten with a little salt and some confectioners' sugar, sugar, 4 apples, pared, cored, and cut in thin slices, mixed with a pinch of sugar, calvados or other compatible liqueur.
In chafing dish pan heat butter, pour in beaten eggs and make the omelette. When omelette is cooked, sprinkle surface with sugar and cover with apple slices. Fold over omelette and place in serving dish, sprinkle with confectioners' sugar. Heat calvados in a small ladle over flame, ignite, and pour the liqueur over the omelette. Serves about 4 to 6 persons.

SUGGESTED WINES:
Asti – Spumante
Champagne

PEACHES OR PEARS FLAMBÉS

Follow directions for Cherries Jubilee (page 179), using peeled fresh peaches or pears if available. Otherwise canned peaches or pears may be used. In which case substitute kirsch for cherry brandy.

SUGGESTED WINES:
Asti – Spumante
Champagne

PEARS FLAMED WITH PORT

Poach pears, pared but left whole, in a mixture of water, sugar and lemon juice. Bring to the chafing dish table with: Butter, sugar, lemon juice, port wine, cognac, blanched almonds, toasted and slivered.

In chafing dish pan, melt butter, then stir in some sugar, lemon juice, and ample port. Cook for a minute or two, add the well-drained pears to the syrup and simmer for about 5 to 10 minutes, turning frequently. Pour over some cognac and ignite. Serve with almonds sprinkled on top.

SUGGESTED WINES:
Asti – Spumante
Champagne

PINEAPPLE CAFÉ DE PARIS

Place in individual containers: Sliced pineapple in its own juice, butter, sugar, cointreau and cognac.

In chafing dish pan melt butter and stir in sugar. Cook until it starts to stick to the bottom, but do not allow it to brown. Stir in some pineapple juice, continue cooking a little longer, add cointreau as well as cognac and ignite. Place pineapple slices in pan and pour flaming liqueur over all.

SUGGESTED WINES:
Asti – Spumante
Champagne

PINEAPPLE FLAMED WITH KIRSCH

Place in individual containers: Thick slices of fresh pineapple, free of rind and core, kirsch, confectioners' sugar, a few cherries.
Place pineapple slices in chafing dish pan. Heat kirsch in a small ladle, and when hot, ignite. Pour over pineapple slices and, while still flaming, sprinkle lavishly with sugar. Garnish each serving with cherries.

SUGGESTED WINES:
Asti – Spumante
Champagne

SCAMPI OR CRAYFISH WITH PERNOD PETIT-DUC

Place in individual containers: Oil, garlic, chopped onion, fine julienne of raw carrots, chopped parsley and tarragon, salt, pepper, cooked scampi or crayfish, peeled and cleaned, cognac, pernod, Sauce Américaine (page 18), cream, consommé.

Into chafing dish pour just enough oil to cover bottom. When very hot, add a sliver of crushed garlic, onion, carrots, herbs, salt, freshly ground pepper, scampi or crayfish. Turn several times. Then sprinkle with ⅓ part cognac and ⅔ part pernod and ignite. Watch out that you don't overdo the spirits. If flame persists, immediately work in sauce américaine, thin it with cream, and a little consommé. Taste for seasoning. Heat well, stirring constantly. Serve in center of a ring of rice.

SUGGESTED WINES:
White Alsatian — Gewürztraminer
White Burgundy — Clos de Vougeot
White — Soave

SEAFOOD SAINT TROPEZ WITH BOURBON

Place in individual containers: Lobster Butter (page 14), julienne of carrots, chopped onions, chopped parsley and tarragon, sliced mushrooms, a sliver of garlic, salt, pepper, fish (prepared in advance), and a combination of any of the following: filets of fish, scampi, mussels, clams, lobsters, scallops, cognac, bourbon, sauce américaine, cream, consommé.

In chafing dish heat lobster butter until it sizzles. Then add carrots, onions, herbs, mushrooms, garlic, salt, freshly ground pepper, and the fish combination which should be drained and warm. Simmer a few minutes. Add ⅓ part cognac, ⅔ part bourbon and ignite. Work in sauce américaine and cream. Thin with a little consommé, if necessary, and sprinkle with a few more drops of bourbon before serving. Taste for seasoning. Serve with rice.

SUGGESTED WINES:
White Burgundy – Clos des Mouches
White Burgundy – Montrachet
White Orvieto – Secco

SHRIMP IN VERMOUTH

For 4 persons cook, peel and clean 1½ pounds shrimp. Bring to the chafing dish in individual containers: Butter, shrimp, dry vermouth, cognac, Velouté (page 28) made with fish stock, cream mixed with egg yolk, sliced, cooked mushrooms, salt, a pepper mill, and chopped parsley.

Melt butter in chafing dish, add shrimp and sauté lightly. Add vermouth, very little cognac, and ignite. Mix in the Velouté, also the cream and egg yolk mixture, mushrooms, salt and freshly ground pepper. Heat through. Sprinkle with parsley before serving.

SUGGESTED WINES:
White Rhine (Hock) – Riesling
White – Soave
Red Rhône – Tavel

RED SNAPPER FLAMED IN HERBS

For this, you need a rather long wire basket that opens in the middle which has short feet on top and bottom so basket can be reversed. Coat a good size, cleaned red snapper, or similar fish, with flour. Make several incisions across the fish and broil until cooked through. Place in the basket, and the basket on a metal tray scattered with fennel, dried thyme, and bay leaves and sprinkle with cognac or anisette. Ignite. After herbs have burned a minute or so, turn basket

and burn a little longer on the other side. Remove fish from basket, skin, debone and serve with Sauce Béarnaise (page 19) on the side.

SUGGESTED WINES:
White Loire – Pouilly-Fumé
White Burgundy – Meursault
White Verdicchio – Castelli di Jesi

FILET OF SOLE MONIQUE

Salt and pepper filets of sole and turn in flour. Place butter in pan and when hot sauté filets till well browned. Remove from pan and keep warm. Place in individual containers sliced mushrooms, coarsely chopped tomatoes, chopped celery, chopped onion, tarragon, Lobster Butter (page 14), lemon juice, cream consommé, red wine and brandy.

In chafing dish heat lobster butter till it sizzles. Add mushrooms, tomatoes, celery, onion, salt, and pepper. Turn several times. Sprinkle with brandy and ignite. Add red wine, a few drops of lemon juice, consommé and cream. Work well and let simmer some 5 minutes. Taste for seasoning. Place filets on serving dish and pour sauce over them. Sauce should be fairly thick.

SUGGESTED WINES:
White Alsatian – Traminer
White Burgundy – Clos de Vougeot
White Burgundy – Montrachet
White – Soave

FILET OF SOLE PRINCESSE

Poach filets in advance, as many as needed, drain, pat dry and keep warm. Place in individual containers: Butter, dry sherry, fine julienne of raw carrots, chopped onion, chopped parsley and tarragon, salt, pepper, cooked, sliced shrimp, sliced mushrooms, French mustard, Velouté made with Fish or Mushroom Stock (page 28), Sabayon (page 18) made with dry white wine, cream, consommé.
In chafing dish heat butter until it starts sizzling, but before taking on color stir in sherry and ignite. Add carrots, onion, herbs, salt, freshly ground pepper, shrimp, mushrooms and French mustard. Blend together well. Simmer for a few minutes, then stir in Velouté, the sabayon and cream. If sauce is too thick (the consistency should not be heavy), add consommé. Mix again well. Pour over the filets, and garnish with rice or boiled potatoes.

SUGGESTED WINES:
White Rhine (Hock) — Deidesheim
White Moselle — Bernkastel
White Bordeaux — Graves

KING CRAB FLAMBÉ

Place in individual containers: Cooked shelled king crab meat, Lobster Butter (page 14), chopped onion, coarsely chopped peeled tomatoes, salt, pepper, dill, chopped celery, sauteéd sliced mushrooms, sour cream, tomato juice, red wine, brandy.

In chafing dish melt lobster butter; when hot add celery, onion, tomatoes, dill, salt, pepper, mushrooms and crab meat. Sprinkle with brandy, ignite. Add red wine, sour cream, tomato juice. Work well. Let simmer about 5 minutes, taste to seasoning. Serve very hot with rice on the side.

SUGGESTED WINES:
White Alsatian – Traminer
White Burgundy – Cos de Vougeot
White Burgundy – Montrachet

STEAK DIANE

Place in individual containers: Butter, chopped onion, parsley and thyme, very thin slices of beef filet (about ¼ inch thick) seasoned with salt and pepper, lemon juice and Worcestershire sauce.
In chafing dish pan melt plenty of butter and when very hot, stir in chopped onion, parsley, and thyme. Cook several minutes until extremely hot, then add the meat and brown quickly on both sides. Add lemon juice and Worcestershire sauce to taste. Remove beef to serving dish and pour over contents from chafing dish pan.
Serve with boiled potatoes or rice and green beans.

SUGGESTED WINES:
Red Rhône – Tavel
Red Beaujolais
Red Burgundy – Beaune

STEAK FLAMBÉ WITH ARMAGNAC

Season the beef filets with salt and press freshly crushed black pepper into the meat on both sides. Take them to the chafing dish table with: Butter, pepper mill, French mustard, armagnac. Sauté the meat in well-heated butter in chafing dish pan to your taste. Add some more fresh butter, ground pepper and spread filets with mustard. Remove pan from flame. Pour armagnac (or cognac) into a small ladle and heat over the flame. Ignite. Return the pan with the steaks to the flame and pour the armagnac over them. As steaks are served spoon liquid from the pan over each one.

SUGGESTED WINES:
Red Bordeaux (Claret) – Médoc
Red Bordeaux (Claret) – Pomerol
Red Bordeaux (Claret) – Saint Emilion
Red Burgundy – Côte de Nuits
Red Burgundy – Pommard

TURBOT MARSEILLAISE

Poach turbot until cooked through, remove skins and bones if any. Drain well, dry, and keep warm. Place in individual containers: Butter, dry sherry or dry vermouth, sliced tomatoes, chopped parsley and tarragon, French mustard, Velouté (page 28) made with fish stock, cream mixed with egg yolk, salt, stock and pepper.
In chafing dish melt butter, stir in some sherry and when hot, ignite. Add tomatoes, parsley, tarragon, a little French mustard, the Velouté, and cream-egg yolk mixture. Season with salt and freshly

ground pepper, add additional sherry or vermouth, if necessary. Pour sauce over turbot, add diced lobster or crab meat and/or mushrooms to sauce, if desired. Serve with rice or boiled potatoes.

SUGGESTED WINES:
White Alsatian – Traminer
White Burgundy – Puligny Montrachet
White – Soave

desserts

The desserts described in this chapter range from such simple family foods as rice pudding with fruit to exotic flaming desserts, soufflés and crêpes of various types. In choosing a recipe for a party it is important to keep in mind the guests one has invited. Women frequently are more interested in low calorie desserts, men in something rich and heavy. The time of day, the climate, and the meal which has preceded should all be given careful thought before the dessert for a party is selected. Also the time available for food preparation is a factor. Some of the desserts may be prepared one or two days in advance, which is definitely an asset in households where little or no domestic help is available.

Exactness of measurements is more important in preparing desserts than in preparing any other types of foods. The amounts of each ingredient going into each dessert are listed as precisely as possible in the recipes which follow. It is not, however, possible to give exact cooking or baking times in most instances. The time required to bake a cake depends on so many factors, among them the size of the pan used, the depth of the batter, and the altitude. The cook must keep a close eye on the dessert as it is baking in order to remove the cake at precisely the correct moment. No cook book can prescribe to the minute the time required for the dessert to reach that optimum. Desserts shouldn't be too sweet or too heavy. For that reason unsweetened chocolate is recommended in all chocolate recipes. Creams and other rich desserts should be served only after comparatively light meals. Fruit desserts are the easiest to digest, and definitely recommended after a particularly rich or heavy main course, especially for luncheons.

VIENNESE CHOCOLATE BISCUITS

Place in your electric mixer the butter and stir until creamy. Add egg yolks, sugar, almonds, flour, melted chocolate, and stir another 10 minutes. Fold in stiffly beaten egg whites. Spread mixture on buttered and floured baking tin about ⅛ of an inch thick and bake in a preheated 350° F oven. When dough begins to shrink away from edges of baking tin, remove from oven and while still hot, cut in strips 1 inch wide and 3 inches long. Cool. Before serving spread red currant jelly on half the strips and top with another strip.

½ cup (1 stick) butter
4 egg yolks
½ cup sugar
⅓ cup grated almonds
½ cup flour
4½ squares (4½ ounces) unsweetened chocolate, melted
4 egg whites
jelly

SUGGESTED WINES:
White Rhine (Hock) — Deidesheim
White Rhine (Hock) — Rüdesheimer
White Bordeaux — Barsac

CHIWAUA CHOCOLATE CAKE

Melt chocolate over hot, but not boiling, water. Beat butter in electric mixer until creamy, then gradually add sugar and continue beating until mixture runs from spoon like a ribbon. Stir in melted chocolate and well-beaten egg yolks and flour. Fold in stiffly beaten egg whites and 4 tablespoons sugar. Pour batter about ⅛ to ¼ inch thick onto a buttered baking sheet. Bake in a preheated 250° F to 300° F oven for about 30 minutes or until cake is done. Remove from oven and, while still warm, cut into 2 equal parts.

- 4 squares (4 ounces) unsweetened chocolate
- ½ cup butter
- ⅔ cup sugar
- 8 egg yolks, well beaten
- ½ cup flour
- 7 egg whites, stiffly beaten

While the cake is baking prepare the following filling:
Melt chocolate over hot, not boiling, water, combine with coffee and heat for a moment or two, remove from heat, and cool. Then add egg yolks and sweetened whipped cream. Mix thoroughly and spread on half of cake. Top with other half of cake and sprinkle lavishly wth confectioners' sugar. Refrigerate until needed. Because the filling is made with whipped cream, cake should be used within 2 days.

FILLING:

- 6½ squares (6½ ounces) unsweetened chocolate
- ½ cup very strong coffee
- 8 egg yolks, well beaten
- 2½ cups heavy cream, whipped and well-sweetened

SUGGESTED WINES:
White Bordeaux – Barsac
Champagne

SACHER CHOCOLATE CAKE

This cake is made without flour. Melt chocolate over hot, but not boiling, water. Mix butter and sugar in electric mixer for about 30 minutes, then add egg yolks and mix another 15 minutes. Stir in chocolate, then zwieback crumbs. Fold in stiffly beaten egg whites. Spoon into a buttered and floured cake mold. Bake in a preheated 300° F oven for about 1 hour. Cool. Turn out of mold and spread top with a layer of red currant jelly or apricot jam. Let set. Cover entire cake with Chocolate Icing (page 14).

9 squares (9 ounces) unsweetened chocolate
1 cup (2 sticks) butter
1 cup sugar
8 egg yolks
⅔ cup zwieback crumbs
12 egg whites, stiffly beaten
Jelly or apricot jam

SUGGESTED WINES:
White Rhine (Hock) – Deidesheim
White Moselle – Bernkastel
White Bordeaux – Barsac

VIENNESE CHOCOLATE CAKE

Melt chocolate over hot, but not boiling, water. Place butter and sugar in electric mixer and beat until creamy. Stir in melted chocolate and egg yolks and mix 10 minutes longer. Then add flour and grated almonds. Continue to mix another 10 minutes. Fold egg whites in carefully and pour batter into buttered and floured high cake mold. Bake in a preheated 350° F oven for 45 to 60 minutes or until done. When cake has cooled slightly remove from mold. When completely cooled cover with Chocolate Icing (page 14).

4 squares (4 ounces) unsweetened chocolate	5 egg yolks, well beaten
½ cup (1 stick) butter	2 tablespoons flour
¾ cup sugar	¾ cup grated almonds
	5 egg whites, stiffly beaten

SUGGESTED WINES:
White Moselle — Bernkastel
White Bordeaux — Barsac
Asti — Spumante

SAND CAKE

Beat butter in electric mixer until creamy. Add sugar, eggs and egg yolks. Beat for 30 minutes. Then add potato flour, rum, grated rind of lemon. Beat 10 to 15 minutes more. Fold in well beaten egg whites, place in buttered cake mold and bake in 250° F oven. Before serving sprinkle with confectioners' sugar.

1 pound (4 sticks) butter	4 cups potato flour
2½ cups confectioners' sugar	2 tablespoons rum
2 whole eggs	Grated lemon rind
7 egg yolks	7 egg whites, stiffly beaten

SUGGESTED WINES:
White Rhine (Hock) — Liebfraumilch
White Loire — Vouvray

SUDANESE CAKE

Place mixing bowl in a pan of simmering water, break eggs into bowl, add sugar and beat with a wire whisk until mixture thickens noticeably. Remove to a pan of cold water and gradually beat in flour. Pour into a buttered, melon-shaped mold and bake in a preheated 350°F oven for about 1 hour or until done. Then remove from oven and cool. Turn out of mold and slice off the top. Hollow out center part of the cake (be careful not to puncture the sides or bottom) and fill with whipped cream. Replace the top and cover entirely with Chocolate Icing (page 14). Serve Raspberry or Strawberry Sauce (page 25) on the side. Serves 6 to 8.

4 eggs
⅔ cup sugar
1 cup all-purpose flour
3 cups cream, whipped
Chocolate icing
Raspberry or strawberry sauce

SUGGESTED WINES:
White Loire — Vouvray
White Bordeaux — Château d'Yquem

desserts

WHITE LADY CAKE

Work butter and sugar together in an electric mixer until creamy. Add egg yolks, almonds, 2 cups whipped cream, rum to taste, and half the cherries. Dip lady fingers slightly one by one in cold milk and arrange compactly over bottom of a rather deep buttered cake mold. Spread a layer of the egg-yolk mixture to a depth of ¼ inch over the lady fingers. Add another layer of milk-dipped lady fingers, repeat the layers until all ingredients are used. Place a heavy weight on top and refrigerate for about 2 hours. Cake can stand overnight if you wish to prepare it in advance. To turn cake out easily, wrap mold with hot, damp cloth and invert quickly on serving plate. Frost with a thin layer of remaining whipped cream, decorate with the remaining cherries.

½ cup (1 stick) butter
⅔ cup sugar
4 egg yolks, well-beaten
¼ pound coarsely chopped almonds
3 cups whipped cream
2 tablespoons rum, about
1 cup diced Maraschino cherries
40-50 lady fingers
Milk

SUGGESTED WINES:
White Bordeaux — Graves
Asti — Spumante

CHARLOTTE MALAKOFF
(DESSERT OF ALMONDS WITH KIRSCH)

In an electric mixer beat ½ cup (1 stick) softened butter and ½ cup granulated sugar until creamy. Stir in 1 cup finely grated unblanched almonds and 2 tablespoons kirsch. Fold in 2 cups whipped cream. Spoon into a lightly oiled charlotte mold and refrigerate until set. To unmold, wrap mold with a hot, damp cloth and turn out quickly on serving dish. Surround the charlotte with lady fingers, pressed lightly against the sides, and pipe whipped cream, with a pastry tube, between the fingers and on the top. Decorate with Maraschino cherries before serving.

SUGGESTED WINES:
White Rhine (Hock) — Liebfraumilch
White Bordeaux — Barsac

STRAWBERRY CHARLOTTE RUSSE

Heat light cream and vanilla bean together until a film shines on top. Beat sugar, egg yolks and whole egg until smooth. Combine with heated cream and cook over boiling water, stirring constantly with a wire whisk, until mixture is well thickened. Sprinkle gelatin over ½ cup cold water, then stir into hot mixture until completely dissolved. Beat over ice until cold. Stir in puréed strawberries, a little Grand Marnier, a few drops of red food coloring, and the whipped cream. Pour into a charlotte mold and refrigerate until firm. To serve, unmold on serving dish and press lady fingers lightly against mold all around. Pipe more whipped cream between lady fingers, if desired.

1 cup light cream
Vanilla bean
½ cup sugar
6 egg yolks
1 whole egg
¾ contents envelope unflavored gelatin
2 cups purée of strawberries
Grand Marnier
Red food coloring
1½ cups whipped cream
Lady fingers

SUGGESTED WINES:
White Moselle – Bernkastel
White Loire – Vouvray
White Bordeaux – Barsac

COUPE BELLE HÉLÈNE

Peel, core, and cut fresh pears in half (tinned pear halves can also be used). Poach the fresh pears in sugar syrup until tender, then drain and cool thoroughly. Make up some Chocolate Sauce (page 20), toast some split, blanched almonds in butter and sprinkle with confectioners' sugar. Cover the bottom of a crystal or silver serving dish with vanilla ice cream. Arrange pear halves on top, then cover the pears with chocolate sauce, hot or cold. Sprinkle with split and toasted almonds.

SUGGESTED WINES:
White Rhine (Hock) – Rüdesheimer
White Moselle – Bernkastel

CRÈME AU CAFÉ

Brown ½ cup sugar lightly. Add ¼ cup milk and put aside. Boil ½ cup milk with a vanilla bean. Cool. Add to this milk, 7 egg yolks and 2 whole eggs, well-beaten. Place the mixing bowl in a pan filled with simmering water. Then add the sugar-milk previously put aside and 1 cup very strong coffee. Beat constantly with wire whisk until the mixture has thickened well. Then take out of the hot water pan, mix in 1 envelope unflavored gelatin which has been softened in ⅓ cup of cold water while the mixture is still hot. Beat over ice until cool. Add strawberries, raspberries or cherries. Fold in 1½ cups whipped cream and pour into serving dish. Decorate with fruit. Place in refrigerator until set. Serve with fruit syrup on the side.

¼ cup sugar
¾ cup milk
Vanilla bean
7 egg yolks plus 2 whole eggs
1 cup very strong coffee
1 envelope unflavored gelatin
Strawberies, raspberries or cherries
1½ cups whipped cream

SUGGESTED WINES:
White Loire – Vouvray
White Bordeaux – Barsac

CRÈME AU CHOCOLAT

Heat milk and vanilla bean together until a film shines on surface. At the same time melt chocolate over hot, but not boiling, water. Beat egg yolks and sugar together until creamy, then stir into milk and cook over boiling water until well thickened. Remove from heat, stir in melted chocolate and gelatin which has been softened in ⅓ cup cold water. When cool, fold in whipped cream and spoon into serving dish. Refrigerate until set. Before serving, decorate with cherries. Serve with canned cherries in their liquid on the side.

2 cups milk
Vanilla bean
5 squares (5 ounces) unsweetened chocolate
6 egg yolks
½ cup sugar
1 envelope unflavored gelatin
2 cups whipped cream
Canned dessert cherries

SUGGESTED WINE:
White Bordeaux – Barsac

CRÈME TRIANON
(VANILLA CREAM WITH MACAROONS)

Heat milk and vanilla bean together until a film shines on top. Beat egg yolks, whole egg, and sugar until creamy. Stir into milk and cook over boiling water, stirring constantly, until well thickened. Sprinkle gelatin over ⅓ cup cold water to soften, then stir into hot milk mixture until dissolved. Add 1 tablespoon kirsch, beat over ice with wire whisk until cold. Fold in whipped cream thoroughly. Soak some macaroons in kirsch and arrange a layer on the bottom of a crystal serving dish. Dot with a little currant jelly and pour a layer of the egg mixture over the macaroons. Cover again with a layer of kirsch-soaked macaroons and continue until all ingredients are used. Refrigerate until set.
Decorate with fresh fruit on top. Serve Raspberry or Strawberry Sauce (page 25) on the side.

3½ cups of milk
Vanilla bean
6 egg yolks
1 whole egg
½ cup of sugar
1 envelope unflavored gelatin
Kirsch
2 cups whipped cream
Macaroons (small)
Red currant jelly
Fresh fruit for decorating
Raspberry or strawberry sauce

SUGGESTED WINES:
White Loire – Vouvray
Asti – Spumante
White Bordeaux – Barsac

desserts

CRÊPES NINA

Make some Crêpes (page 11). For each crêpe chop 8 to 10 hazelnuts roughly. Fry slightly in butter and sugar, sprinkle with Grand Marnier and ignite. Then add some fresh raspberries or strawberries and a little more Grand Marnier. Mix well and fill crêpes. Fold over once, sprinkle with confectioners' sugar, and glaze under the broiler.

SUGGESTED WINES:
White Rhine (Hock) – Deidesheim
White Rhine (Hock) – Riesling
Champagne

CRÊPES TYROLIENNE

Make Crêpes (page 11), fill with apricot jam, fold over once, sprinkle with confectioners' sugar and toasted split almonds. Set under broiler to glaze.

SUGGESTED WINES:
White Rhine (Hock) – Riesling
White Moselle – Piesporter
Champagne

PÊCHE MELBA

Skin fresh peaches, cut in half, and poach in sugar syrup until tender (tinned peach halves can be used in place of fresh). Drain and cool. Put scoops of vanilla ice cream in the bottoms of individual dessert dishes, place ½ peach on top of each and cover with Raspberry or Strawberry Sauce (page 25). Decorate with whipped cream and/or toasted, slivered almonds.

SUGGESTED WINE:
White Bordeaux – Château d'Yquem

FRUIT DESSERT

For 4 to 6 servings, mix together well 5 egg yolks, 5 tablespoons sugar, 2 tablespoons flour and stir well. Add juice of 1 lemon, then add a purée of fresh raspberries or strawberries (about 1 pound of the raw, clean fruit). Place all ingredients in a saucepan, beating constantly over a low flame until it thickens, then remove from fire and fold in 4 stiffly beaten egg whites. Should the color seem very pale, add a few drops of red food coloring. Pour into serving dish and chill.

SUGGESTED WINES:
White Loire – Vouvray
White Bordeaux – Barsac

LADIES' KISSES

Beat ½ cup softened butter with ¼ cup sugar in electric mixer until creamy. Then, with your hand, knead in thoroughly 1 egg yolk, 1⅓ cups flour. Form a ball and refrigerate for about 1 hour. Pinch off portions of dough and shape into balls the size of a walnut, dip into beaten egg, then roll in coarsely chopped almonds. Place on a buttered baking sheet and press a little indentation in each ball with

your finger. Bake in a preheated 350° F oven until light brown and baked through.
After cookies have cooled place a little dab of red currant jelly in the indentation immediately before serving.

SUGGESTED WINES:
White Loire — Vouvray
White Bordeaux — Barsac
Champagne

LOGANBERRIES OR RASPBERRIES A L'ORIENTALE

Wash and drain loganberries or raspberries. Place in a bowl and mix with coarsely chopped nuts and/or crushed meringues. Mix some sour cream with sugar, add a little coffee or cocoa liqueur. Pour over the fruit, place a layer of vanilla or coffee ice cream on the bottom of a crystal dish. Pour berry mixture over the top.

SUGGESTED WINES:
White Loire — Vouvray
White Bordeaux — Barsac

MOUSSE AU CHOCOLAT

Beat 6 egg yolks and ½ cup sugar together with an electric mixer until mixture drops from a spoon like a string. Stir in 1½ cups unsweetened melted chocolate, then fold in 3 cups whipped cream. Spoon into individual dessert dishes or a bowl and chill.

SUGGESTED WINE:
White Bordeaux — Barsac

PEARS À LA RITZ

Peel some pears leaving them whole. Poach in sugar syrup until tender, but still shapely. When cool slice off about ⅓ from the stem end, scoop out core and pits very carefully and turn upside down to drain. Melt some unsweetened chocolate over hot water and mix with a little cream and sugar. Fill cavity of each pear with the chocolate mixture and cover with the stemmed top. Place pears on serving dish and pour a somewhat thick Vanilla Sauce (page 27) over pears. Serve well chilled.

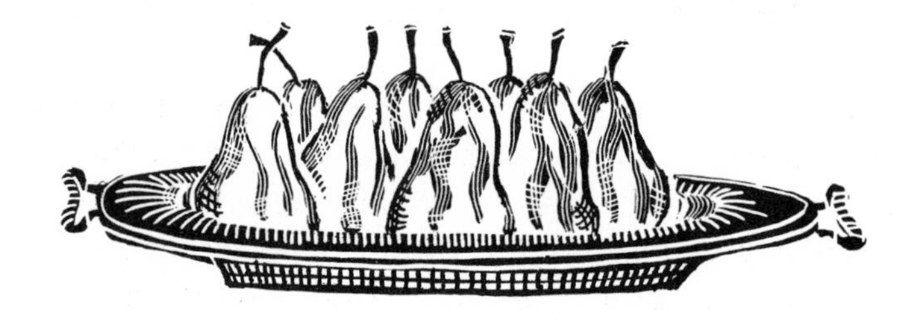

SUGGESTED WINES:
White Bordeaux — Barsac
Champagne

FRUIT PIE

Sift 3 cups flour and a pinch of salt into a bowl. Work in ¾ cup butter and ½ tablespoon oil until dough holds together. Rest in the refrigerator for about 1 hour. Fill a large deep-dish pan with slices of pared apples. The dish should be full to the brim. Sprinkle with sugar, raisins and apricot jam, and pour over ½ cup white wine and ½ cup water. Roll out pastry, cover apples completely and press down to the rim to seal securely. Brush the pastry generously with beaten egg, then sprinkle with granulated sugar. Bake in preheated 425° F oven for about 45 minutes. (Note: any fruit suitable for pie may be used.)

3 cups all-purpose flour	Sugar
Salt	Raisins
¾ cup butter (1½ sticks)	Apricot jam
½ tablespoon vegetable oil	½ cup white wine
Apples	Egg

SUGGESTED WINES:
White Moselle – Bernkastel
White Bordeaux – Margaux
Champagne

POT DE CRÈME AU CHOCOLAT

Combine 3 cups of milk or half cream and half milk with ½ cup sugar and 4 squares (4 ounces) unsweetened chocolate. Cook over low heat, stir until chocolate melts and mixture is well blended. Remove from heat and cool. Beat in 6 egg yolks, one at a time, beating hard after each addition. Then beat in 1 whole egg, strain twice through a fine strainer and pour into individual dessert cups. Place cups in a pan of hot water and simmer on top of stove until mixture has set. Be careful that none of the water splashes into the mixture. Refrigerate. Before serving, sprinkle with grated chocolate. Serves about 6.

PROFITEROLLES AUX FRAMBOISES

Make Dough for Cream Puffs (page 15). Fill with whipped cream and cover generously with a rather thick Raspberry or Strawberry Sauce (page 25).

PROFITEROLLES AU CHOCOLAT

Proceed as for profiterolles aux framboises, but cover with Chocolate Sauce (page 20) instead of fruit sauce.
A very decorative and tasteful presentation is achieved by serving both types of profiterolles in two separate serving dishes (referred to as profiterolles rouges et noirs).

SUGGESTED WINES:
White Loire — Vouvray
White Bordeaux — Barsac
Champagne

BREAD AND BUTTER PUDDING

Heat milk until a film shines on surface. Set aside to cool. When lukewarm stir in eggs, salt, sugar, and most of the raisins. Pour into a buttered baking dish, cover top with slices of white bread from which the crusts have been removed. Sprinkle top with additional sugar, remaining raisins, and dot with butter. Place dish in a pan of simmering water and bake in a preheated 350° F oven for about 45 minutes.

1 quart milk
4 eggs, well beaten
Pinch salt
2 tablespoons sugar
½ cup raisins
Sliced white bread
Butter

SUGGESTED WINE:
White Bordeaux – Barsac

TAPIOCA PUDDING

Combine milk and tapioca, cook over very low heat for about 10 minutes. Remove from stove and stir in sugar. When cooled slightly, add raisins and egg yolks. Place over hot water and cook, stirring constantly, for about 5 minutes. Transfer to buttered baking dish, set dish in a pan of simmering water and bake in a preheated 350°F oven for about 15 minutes or until top is lightly brown.

1 quart of milk
7 tablespoons tapioca
⅔ cup sugar
½ cup raisins
6 egg yolks, well beaten

Serve with chilled stewed fruit.

SUGGESTED WINES:
White Loire – Sancerre
White Bordeaux – Barsac

RICE WITH FRUIT

Heat milk and vanilla bean until a film shines on the surface. Stir in rice, sugar and salt and cook over a low heat until rice is tender. Sprinkle gelatin over ¼ cup cold water to soften, remove rice from heat, stir in gelatin until dissolved. Cool. Fold in whipped cream and spoon mixture into a buttered ring mold. Refrigerate until firm. Unmold on serving dish and fill center with mixed, stewed fruit.

2½ cups milk
Vanilla bean
1 cup uncooked rice
½ cup of sugar
Pinch salt
½ envelope unflavored gelatin
1½ cups whipped cream
Stewed fruit

SUGGESTED WINES:
White Loire — Vouvray
White Bordeaux — Barsac

SCHMARRN

Combine 4 tablespoons butter with sugar and flour. Place in electric mixer. Beat until creamy, then add egg yolks and beat a few minutes longer. Stir in raisins and almonds, fold in stiffly beaten egg whites carefully. Melt remaining butter in a large, heavy, iron skillet. Add batter, work a spatula around edge of skillet for a few minutes, then place in preheated 450° F oven until bottom is well browned. Flip over with a broad spatula and brown the other side. Remove from oven and while still hot, tear into small pieces with 2 forks, sprinkle with confectioners' sugar. Serve hot with cold applesauce or other stewed fruit on the side.

- 7 tablespoon of butter for batter
- 3 tablespoons sugar
- 2 tablespoons flour
- 3 egg yolks
- ½ cup raisins
- ½ cup slivered almonds
- 3 egg whites, stiffly beaten
- Confectioners' sugar
- Applesauce

SUGGESTED WINES:
White Loire – Vouvray
White Bordeaux – Barsac

ENGLISH SOUP (MIXED FRUITS, SPONGE CAKE, AND MERINGUE)

Prepare batter for Génoise (page 16) and bake in a large, shallow baking pan. The cake should be about ½-inch thick when baked. In the bottom of a large, oven-proof serving dish (dish should be not less than 3 inches deep), place a 1½ inch layer of mixed fruit.

Part of the fruit should be uncooked: (strawberries, apples, raspberries, sections of orange and/or grapefruit, pineapple); part should be cooked (plums, pears, cherries, to name a few). Whatever fruits you use, they should be cut to approximately the same size. Drain thoroughly and sprinkle with sugar, kirsch or rum. Cut the layer of Génoise exactly the size of the serving dish and place on top of the fruit. Mix together a few tablespoons Crème Pâtissière (page 18) with some confectioners' sugar, a little kirsch or rum, and about 3 times the amount of stiffly beaten egg whites as you have crème pâtissière. Spread a ¼ to ½ inch layer on top of the Génoise. On top of this pipe, through a pastry bag, a covering of stiffly beaten egg whites mixed with ample confectioners' sugar. Sprinkle with confectioners' sugar, place under a preheated broiler to take on a golden color. Refrigerate and serve well chilled.

SUGGESTED WINE:
Asti – Spumante

SOUFFLÉ CABARET

For each person, take 2 heaping tablespoons thick Crème Pâtissière (page 18), heat to lukewarm, stir in 2 egg yolks, and about 1 tablespoon shaved, unsweetened chocolate. To this mixture add a little Grand Marnier or any other orange-base liqueur. Beat 2 egg whites until practically dry, gradually adding 3 tablespoons confectioners' sugar. Fold egg whites carefully into original mixture and spoon into individual soufflé dishes that have been buttered and lightly coated with sugar. Fill to about 4/5 of capacity. Sprinkle with confectioners' sugar, place under a hot broiler for a moment to form a slight skin, then into a preheated 400° F oven for 10 minutes. Reduce oven heat to 300° F and continue baking until soufflés are well cooked around the edges, but still somewhat creamy in the center. Take to the table quickly. Now, with 2 forks, bake a hole in the center of each soufflé and pour in ½ to 1 tablespoon flaming orange liqueur. NOTE: Soufflés may be prepared in individual molds or large molds sufficient for up to 6 persons. Obviously, the larger the mold, the longer the baking time. Approximate sizes of molds are indicated with recipe for Soufflé of Oysters (page 96).

SUGGESTED WINE:
Champagne

CHOCOLATE SOUFFLÉ I

For 2 persons beat 2 egg yolks and 2 tablespoons sugar in the electric mixer until mixture drops from spoon like a string. Melt 1½ squares (1½ ounces) unsweetened chocolate over hot water. Stir into eggs along with ½ tablespoon flour. Fold in 3 stiffly beaten egg whites. Coat bottom and sides of a small soufflé dish lightly with butter and granulated sugar. Pour in chocolate mixture and bake in a preheated 400° F oven for about 20 to 25 minutes. After 10 minutes reduce heat to 325° F. Sprinkle with confectioners' sugar and serve immediately.

SUGGESTED WINES:
White Bordeaux – Barsac
Champagne – Brut

CHOCOLATE SOUFFLÉ II

For 4 persons melt 3 squares (3 ounces) unsweetened chocolate over hot water. Make a Béchamel Sauce (page 10) with 1½ tablespoons butter, 1½ tablespoons flour, and hot milk. The Béchamel should be fairly thick. Add 6 tablespoons sugar, combine with the Béchamel and cool. Stir in 3 egg yolks, 1 tablespoon hot milk. Mix well. Then fold in 5 stiffly beaten egg whites. Butter a medium-size soufflé dish on all sides and sprinkle with granulated sugar. Pour in chocolate mixture and bake in a preheated 400°F oven for about 30 minutes. Reduce heat to about 325°F after 10 minutes. The soufflé should be well done around the rim and still somewhat creamy in the center. Sprinkle with confectioners' sugar and serve immediately.

SUGGESTED WINES:
White Moselle – Bernkastel
White Bordeaux – Barsac
Asti – Spumante

CRÊPES SOUFFLÉS

For 4 persons make 4 Crêpes (page 11) somewhat larger than directed in recipe. Prepare a mixture of Soufflé Grand Marnier (page 224)—half the quantity in the recipe is sufficient—and spoon thickly on each crêpe. Fold over once. Make 2 or 3 small incisions in the top of each crêpe. Now take stiffly beaten egg whites, sweetened with plenty of confectioners' sugar, and pipe strips crosswise on top of each crêpe. Sprinkle with toasted almond slivers, place in a but-

tered oven-proof serving dish, and slide under a preheated broiler for a moment until delicately brown. Transfer quickly to a preheated 450°F oven for 6 to 8 minutes or until soufflé mixture inside the crêpes has puffed. Sprinkle with confectioners' sugar and serve at once.

SUGGESTED WINE:
White Bordeaux – Barsac

OMELETTE SOUFFLÉ

This dish must be worked very rapidly so get all ingredients ready beforehand. Beat 3 egg yolks thoroughly. In a separate bowl beat 6 egg whites, gradually adding 1 cup of confectioners' sugar while beating. When egg whites are well beaten mix with egg yolks. Spoon mixture into a pastry bag, place very hard ice cream (whatever flavor you prefer) onto an oven-proof serving dish. Mound egg mixture on top in a decorative fashion, sealing the ice cream completely on all sides. Sprinkle with sugar. Place in a preheated 500° F oven until slightly brown. Garnish all around with a mixture of fruits (whatever is in season), bring immediately to the table, sprinkle the fruit with kirsch, ignite and serve.

SUGGESTED WINES:
White Rhine (Hock) – Deidesheim
White Moselle – Bernkastel
Champagne

SOUFFLÉ GRAND MARNIER

For 2 persons take 4 heaping tablespoons lukewarm Crème Pâtissière (page 18), add a little Grand Marnier and some confectioners' sugar. Beat in 4 egg yolks thoroughly. Beat 4 egg whites until practically dry, adding ample confectioners' sugar while beating. Fold gently into egg yolk mixture. Butter a small soufflé dish on all sides and sprinkle lightly with granulated sugar. Spoon in soufflé mixture to about ¾ the capacity of the mold. Sprinkle top quickly with Grand Marnier, then with confectioners' sugar. Place under a preheated broiler just long enough to give it a slight skin. Bake in a preheated 400° F oven for about 18 to 22 minutes, or until the edge is well-baked, but the center still somewhat creamy.

SUGGESTED WINES:
White Bordeaux – Château d'Yquem
Champagne

SHELL FOR FRUIT TARTS

Work ½ cup butter with 1¼ cups flour, then add 5 tablespoons sugar and 1 egg yolk. Work again, then allow to rest in refrigerator for 30 minutes. Roll out on buttered and floured baking tin about ⅛ inch thick and bake in a 350° F oven until beginning to turn slightly brown. Take out of oven. Place fresh fruit or preserved fruit on the shell (optional: sprinkle the fruit with grated almonds), then replace in oven and bake until done.

TART STEPHANIE

Place butter in electric mixer together with sugar, beat until creamy. Add almonds, egg yolks, grated rind of lemon. Stir well. Add zwieback crumbs which have been soaked in white wine. Mix in cinnamon to taste. Fold in stiffly beaten egg whites. Place batter on buttered, lightly floured baking pan, top with sour cherries (fresh or canned). Bake in preheated 350° F oven.

½ cup (1 stick) butter
½ cup sugar
½ cup unblanched almonds, grated with skins
6 eggs
Lemon rind
½ cup zwieback crumbs
White wine
Cinnamon
Cherries

SUGGESTED WINES:
White Burgundy — Puligny-Montrachet
Asti — Spumante

index

index

index

index